Guiding Light Verses

Spiritual and Inspirational

Verses for Life's Journey

Written by Sue Hicks

with her Inspirers in Spirit

Compiled and Designed by Oliver Carpenter-Beale

Dedication

Dedicated to my Dad, the font of all knowledge before the advent of Google, and David Jarvis, who helped me to persevere with my efforts to communicate with Spirit until it finally dawned on me that all I needed to do was pick up a pen. Both of you have the patience of saints!

Love and Light

Sue x

About the author

I am a member of Hastings Spiritualist Brotherhood Church and began writing poems and channelled guidance several years ago.

The purpose of this work is to bring comfort and understanding to those in need or wishing to learn more about spiritual matters. The words do not necessarily represent my thoughts on any particular subject. They flow from the end of the pen without much interference from me, in fact the less thought I put into it the better the final result.

The words I have written have given me a better understanding of how life needs to be lived in order to get the most from the experience. I have been left firmly convinced that we are a spirit residing in a physical body whose existence continues after our death. While we are here on earth assistance is available to us if only we remember to ask for it. I hope these words bring the same clarity and understanding to those who read them.

Sue Hicks

Contents

The Scribe

Do my words carry any meaning for you?
Do they make cogs whirr and pennies drop?
Do they bring forth emotions, laughter or tears?

If they resonate with you so that you feel you own them,
Then claim them for your own, as if they are meant only for you.

Use them for guidance, for comfort, for support.
Keep them close to you or share them far and wide.
Do not assume they represent my thoughts, my feelings, my beliefs.

They appear on the page before me as I write.
They turn up when I least expect.
My task is to record them as they fall from my head.

I am merely the scribe.

Be Patient

Many are the times we have given up trying.
Trying to solve insoluble problems.
We become dragged into a spiral of despair.
We seek solutions that never come.
The harder we try the bigger the disappointment.
We pick ourselves up, we try again.
Only to be kicked again as we fall down.
Frustration drives us to the point of insanity.
We consider more reckless, more unlikely solutions.
These too are doomed to fail.
Some things are not meant to be.
Others take their own sweet time.
Meanwhile we need the patience of a saint.
Step away for a while from the insoluble.
Seek solace in the little things that heal.
Spend time in nature; watch the changes of the seasons.
Nature has patience.
It waits until the time is right for things to happen.
Then things will bloom and new life appear.
Life moves on.
So it will be for us.
When the time is right, life will move on.
Be patient.

Beacon of Light

*H*ow can we demonstrate that life is worth living to those who have no desire to live?

What can we do to stop them focusing on the darkness? There is no magic answer, they are all where they are for different reasons...but they must all have something positive in their lives that they can cling to, that will hold them here and prevent them from taking a path of no return.

It may be the smallest thing that they can focus on but you can find it and hold it out to them like a beacon.
Show them the beauty of nature, take them outside into the world we provide and let it lift their spirit.

Let them connect with the animal kingdom; let it show them the love that they lack.

Do not let them become isolated, keep them connected to this world and surround them with love.

They still have work to do here; it is not yet their time.

Confidence

Confidence is the key to performance.
Without it you are not believable.
You must believe in yourself first and then others will believe in you too.

They will be caught up in your ability to carry them to another place.

To feel their troubles slip away as they escape into the world you create.

How do you develop into a confident performer?
Ironically, in order to become confident you must do that which you fear.
Conquer the fear and you will become a confident performer.

Fear is a necessary emotion to protect us from harm.
It prevents us from jumping off cliffs, climbing without ropes, swimming in unknown waters.
This keeps us safe, keeps us alive.

In the world of performance we do not need fear to keep us safe.
It does not enhance our work; it merely prevents us from stepping before an audience.

Imagine how far you could go in a world without fear.
What would you do if you had no fear?

Conflict

Conflict surrounds you.
Do not be frightened by it.
It has always been thus.
Do not be frightened to step outside.
Do not fear engaging with others.
It is by engaging that you will become known.
Be known to others and let them be known to you.
Understand the ways of others.
Let others understand your ways.
Explain your ideals.
Explain your philosophy.
Let it be known that you will tolerate the philosophy of others.
But in tolerating others make it known that you expect tolerance in return.
There is no right way to be.
Just a way that you can live with.
Find this way for yourself.
Do not let others impose their ways upon you.
Listen by all means.
For in listening comes understanding.
Make sure that you are heard in return that you may educate others.
Drive ignorance out of the intolerant.
Replace it with love, light and understanding
That is the way forward.
That is the path of peace.

Deceit

To deceive is a common flaw of the human state.
It is sometimes done to protect others from hurt.
More often it is done to protect the perpetrator of a misdemeanour.

The truth has a way of surfacing at a later time.
Much time may pass before it resurfaces but be sure Spirit will ensure that it has the opportunity to do so.
Deceit only serves to delay dealing with one's responsibilities.
It is better to face the consequences of one's actions sooner rather than later.

Others will think better of you for your honesty.
It will provide the opportunity to learn and grow.
Sometimes the most deceitful are those who deceive themselves.

They refuse to see the consequences of their actions.
They make excuses for their behaviour or bury their heads in the sand.

It is not possible to force someone to face up to their deceit.
That decision must come from within and will take courage.

Only then can the soul learn.
Only then can it grow.

Earth Angel Prayer

Let the light of the world shine upon you.
Let it reflect from you and illuminate dark corners.
May you be a beacon of light for others to follow.

Bringing healing where there is pain.
Bringing reconciliation where there is conflict.
Bringing joy where there is misery.
Bringing hope where there is despair.

May you help other souls discover the causes of their anguish.
May you give them the wisdom to see the changes that will alter their path.

May you provide the courage to take the first steps.
May you eliminate the fear of the unknown that holds back the progress of so many.

May you teach others to trust in the journey and not fear the obstacles which strew their path.

May you lead by example so that others may follow.

Know that Spirit will guide you until the end of your journey.

Emotionally Speaking

Sentiments, feelings, emotions are placed over you while you are here.
These are to make you engage with your journey.
Without them you would live life in a state of limbo.
No progress would be made without the emotions to drive you forwards.
You would continue to live, but in a passionless life.
Nothing would drive you, motivate you.
You would exist day to day, that is true.
You would survive in a life of nothingness.
No anger, no greed, no happiness, no desire to meet your needs.
No love to pull you towards another soul, whether human or animal.
You would live in isolation and would not care that it were so.
Do not fear the emotions we send you.
Do not fear to engage with them.
Engage wholeheartedly, with every fibre of your being.
They are meant to be felt and felt deeply.
Do not brush them aside as if they do not matter.
They are the only thing that matters.
They are your reason to be.
They are your reason to live.
Enjoy the feelings that they bring forwards.
Do not fear them but learn from the experiences they cause you to engage with.
If you do not like the feelings that certain emotions evoke in you then seize the opportunity to change your situation to rid yourself of them.
Then you will progress.

Empathy

The ability to empathise with others can be a great gift.
But it can also be a curse.
It is easy to absorb the emotions of those around you.
Being around happy people makes you feel happy.
Being around sad people makes you feel sad.
Being with angry people can make you feel angry.
So many emotions we can feel from others, how can we tell which feelings are our own?
How does our true, authentic self, feel?
We must separate ourselves from others sometimes.
It serves us well to have time alone.
Then we can connect with our true inner self and examine our own emotions.
We can choose how we feel.
We see people who are happy despite the trials that life has brought them.
They have chosen to be happy.
We see people who are miserable, angry, envious or full of hate for no good reason.
They have chosen to dwell with those emotions.
Those emotions may become habits that are hard to break.
If others with these emotions surround you, you should seek the solitude of your own being.
Banish the emotional burden of others for a time and become yourself again.
Then seek out the company of those who will lift your spirit, even if only for a while.
You cannot choose how the people around you feel.
But you can choose not to feel like them.

For the Healers

Step forward, out of the darkness and into the light.
Step forward with us that we may lead you in the ways of healing.
You cannot quantify the healing energy.
You cannot apply the rules and regulations that you love so much to the application of spirit energy.
You try to define the parameters for healing energy, try to regulate its application.
These things are not for you to decide.
You are merely a conduit via which we can work.
You allow us to use your body as a tool, an instrument through which we can channel the forces of Spirit.
You may ask us to direct the energy to where it is required.
You may ask us to direct it to a recipient whether person or animal.
You cannot control the outcome; that is for us to decide in communication with the recipient.
The recipient of your choosing may choose to deny the healing in order to fulfil their life's path.
The application of healing may delay the inevitable and that may not be their choice.
Your intentions are of the highest and sent in love but you cannot heal that which chooses not to be healed.
You may view these as your failures but know that the failure was not yours nor was it Spirit's.
Celebrate your successes for they will be many and much valued.
Bring healing to the many that are willing to receive and feel no guilt for those that are not.

Freedom

Freedom is something that we take for granted.
The freedom to walk down the street when we choose.
The freedom to travel to other parts of the world.
The freedom to form relationships with the partners of our choice.
The freedom to be educated regardless of our gender.
These are freedoms that our ancestors fought hard for.
They should be guarded fiercely and not eroded as a result of apathy or complacency.
Those who try to destroy these freedoms should be shouted down.
They would impose on you their own standards which belong to another age.
Your ancestors had long moved away from such beliefs.
They had learned the restrictions that these beliefs bring do not serve the development of the human soul.
Men and women should be allowed to develop equally.
The one gender should not impose their standards upon the other.
There should be no need to control another human being; they came here capable of making their own decisions, with their own journey to undertake.
It is not the place of one human being to control the path of another.
Guard your freedom well; do not let it be taken away from you by stealth or by force.

Ghost

I am a shadow of my former self,
An image left behind in the ether.
It represents what I was, not what I am now.
Like looking at a photograph of a time gone by.
Do not be afraid of this image, it cannot hurt you.
I am no longer there, I have moved on to better things.
It represents my energy, an imprint left by an extraordinary event.
An event that shocked me so deeply that it left its imprint for all time,
To linger on into the future for others to see and feel.
Engage with it if you must, it can do you no harm.
Carry out your experiments; use your instruments to measure.
Sense the energy of my misfortune that you may feel it too.
But know that I am not trapped there.
I do not need rescuing, you can leave me be.
My soul has moved along its path as it should.
And I am where I am meant to be.
Surrounded by love.

Go Forward

Go forward into the universe.
It will rise to greet you.
It will bring forward great truths and open your mind to many possibilities.
That which you thought could not be achieved will come to you as if by magic.
Release the barriers that hold you back for they exist only in your imagination.
All things are achievable.
There are no impossibilities.
Time will expand to allow all things to happen.
That which must be done, will be done.
That which must come to pass, will come to pass.
That which must be suffered, will be suffered.
Therein lies the secret of all learning.
Therein lies progress.
It is only through progress that you will reach enlightenment.
All the sufferings will be distant memories.
Do not fear what we send to challenge you.
Your fear will paralyse you, prevent your action.
Trust that the challenges are necessary.
There are no pointless tasks.
You can choose to engage or not.
The decisions are yours.
Do not fear the engagement.
We will bring the support you require at the designated time.
All things will become apparent as you progress.
But you must progress to make things apparent.
The best thing to do is start.
If there are no beginnings there can be no endings.

Gratitude

We should be grateful for the abundance we have in our lives.
We have enough to eat, clothes to wear and safe places to live.
Many who travel this Earthly path with us do not have those privileges.
They suffer greatly during their journey, yet even amidst the suffering they learn to be grateful for the small things that they are blessed with.
The love of family, of partners and friends.
The love of animals.
The ability to enjoy the beauty of this world.
A sunset or the moon at night or the patterns of the stars in the sky.
We have so much in our lives that these souls do not, yet still we are discontented.
You are not here to have the perfect life and should stop seeking it.
You are here to experience a myriad of emotions and events.
Not all of these will be positive but the negative should make you appreciate the positive all the more.
Be grateful for what you have and stop yearning for things that were never meant to be.

Guidance

Guidance is something that we seek all the time.
We seek advice from friends, family, anyone who will listen.
We look things up, read, research,
Anything to help us reach a decision.
We can ask for so much advice that we end up confused and overwhelmed by the amount of information we have tried to take on board.
But often the answer to a question lies within us.
We should trust our instincts, our gut feelings.
Our head and our heart can be influenced by others but our gut is always true to us.
If something feels like a bad idea it is probably a bad idea.
If you feel passionate about something, if you can't stop thinking about it, if thinking about it makes you happy then you should pursue it.
Find a way to make it happen, do not be afraid of the consequences, do not fear failure.
The wherewithal to achieve your dreams will appear before you once you have taken the first step.
But if you do not take the first step it will remain but a dream.

Healing

A channel as wide as the ocean, open and of pure intent, seeking only to relieve the suffering of others is all we require for healing to take place.
The energy will flow freely from angelic realms when its presence is asked for.
Those who feel undeserving will block the flow of this energy; prevent their own healing from taking place however much we feel they deserve to be healed.
Many souls block their own healing in this way, punishing themselves unnecessarily.
We will send healing to any soul that needs it.
There are no undeserving souls.
The events that have been experienced by souls in this incarnation can make them resist our efforts to bring healing into their lives.
If they have watched others suffer then they may feel that they deserve to suffer too.
We do not see that any soul should be denied healing.
It is open to all.
If you ask, we will provide, if you need, we will provide.
But you must be prepared to receive and accept that you deserve to be healed.

Heaven

Whence did thou come?
Wouldst thou know?
Thou shalt return to that state once thy time here is complete.
The start and the finish are one and the same.
Birth and death merely portals through which we pass to and from the same state of being.
The realms beyond the physical state inhabited here are infinite and yours to create.
Leave the preconceptions behind you when you leave this place and you can make your own heaven unconstrained by the beliefs imposed upon you by the leaders that you follow here.
Do not let their limited visions limit the realms that you can create for yourself.
Follow your leaders by all means.
They bring structure to your life and answers to your questions.
Rules to live life by, bringing stability to your world.
But do not assume that their way is the only way.
There are many ways to be.
It does not matter which one you follow or if you follow one at all.
Know that these beliefs limit you.
The ideas that you explore here will open you up to greater possibilities.
There are no limits for these possibilities and they will allow you to expand your ideas without limit when you return whence you came.

Higher Self

At one with all things, all seeing, all knowing, guiding the hands of their allocated soul.

An enabler, putting the thoughts into the mind that will drive the soul forwards on their path.
No physical form, pure energy, capable of linking back into the universal consciousness and bringing forth information to link with the allocated soul.

There are those who ignore the guidance of the higher self, refuse to accept that help is available, do not listen to the inner voice that tries to guide their hand.
Why would you not avail yourself of the services of your higher self?
They are an extension of you.
Use them to examine your faults, become self-critical and look at yourself from the outside.

Try to see yourself as others see you.
For yourself, try not to control every situation, give your problems to Spirit, allow them provide the answers.

Your higher self will act as a conduit for the answers to find their way back to you.

Your Word

Hold fast to your beliefs, they are your beliefs for good reason.
You do not follow blindly, the fashion of the season.
You have worked things out, you have studied well,
Your thoughts your own, not what others tell
You, you should believe. Your mind’s your own,
Not a field where other's ideas were sown.
An original soul, not a clone, one of many,
Your thoughts are unique, not ten for a penny.
If you've something to say, it needs to be heard,
Never underestimate the power of your word.
Go forward, reach out, put your words before others,
Have the courage to speak to your sisters and brothers.
They need you to speak so that they may then hear,
Words of guidance, of comfort, to allay what they fear.
Bring humour with you to lighten the word,
It will make others listen, so the message is heard.

History Repeats

The teachings of our prophets should be heeded.
You should have already learned this lesson but you make the same mistakes over again.

Look at the history that has gone before.
It contains all the knowledge that you need.
You must speak out, look at unfair situations and bring a voice of reason to the argument.

Do not let bigotry go unchallenged.
There are many misguided, misinformed souls voicing opinions that will lead to pain for the innocent.
Bring clarity to others.
Staying silent is not an option.

It is what others did before you and it allows the madman to rule the sane.
You must have the courage to speak out and others will join you.

Keep pointing to the past, draw attention to the similarities in today's events. The evidence is there to support your assertions, so much evidence that only a fool could ignore it.

But the world is full of fools who would lead the wise if the wise are foolish enough to let them.

Intelligence

The most intelligent people may regard themselves as superior to others on the Earth plane.
But that is not the case.
Spirit values each soul equally.
The less intelligent should not feel inferior.
They have chosen a harder path through life.
The intelligent have brought with them tools that the less intelligent do not have access to.
These may make their path easier as they are capable of dealing with the trials that life brings.
Some will use their intelligence to serve and to ease the path of others.
But some will use it to make others subordinate and take advantage of them.
That is not a good use of the tools we provide.
It will not serve their soul's purpose in this life.
They will not learn.
They will not rise in our estimation.
They will return to Spirit having achieved nothing.
A lifetime wasted.
Sometimes those less intelligent souls appear to make no progress on the Earth plane.
You watch them struggle with simple tasks.
You cannot see a point to their lives.
They must be helped with all that they attempt.
You should look at them and count your blessings.
They are not here to learn.
They are here to teach.

Ignorance

Do not deride the ignorant, no person can know all things.
Different cultures have different customs, different rules.
You do not know all the different ways that humans choose to be.

So many cultures, so many customs, so many interpretations of Spirit.

It is easy to cause offence because of ignorance.
Should that ignorance be punished, should it be ridiculed?
Should it be allowed to escalate until bloodshed ensues?
Surely ignorance should lead to education?

Explain your ways and encourage others to explain theirs.
Thereby lies understanding, thereby lies tolerance.
Our many cultures have much in common.
We should seek the common ground, not exploit the differences.
Those who would point the finger and ridicule or attack should be taught respect.
As they would have others respect their ways.
It is not the job of others to be the teacher.

We should not allow intolerance to go unchallenged.
We should have the courage to educate the ignorant.
To raise our voices when those around us remain silent.
To encourage peace and harmony as the way forward.

Learn to Trust, Trust to Learn

We know not what goes on in the minds of others.
We are not privy to their innermost thoughts.
We only see the face they are prepared to show us.
No matter how well we think we know someone, we never really know them at all.

They may put on a show of confidence when inside there is none.
They may hide their fears from us.
They may hide their pain.
They may hide behind a facade of respectability when inside lies evil.
They may hide their true intent behind a mask of friendliness.

How can we tell what lies inside?
The simple answer is that we cannot.
We have to trust our instincts, our gut feeling.
This is guidance from above, from our higher self.
Listen to those feelings, do not block them.
If there is doubt, walk away.

But do not let bad experiences stop you from trusting again.
Without trust, there can be no true friendships, no true loves.

Take a leap into the unknown.
Good or bad, you will learn much from the experience.

I Will

I will refuse to bow to the pressures this world pours upon me, I will take time out to do the things my head needs to do.

I will take time to sleep, to recharge, to repair the damage done by the thoughts of the day.
Allow my brain to be cleansed by my dreams, wiping away the trials that plague me.
Escape from this world awhile, play another game with different rules, different players.

I will take time to think, put my thoughts in order so I can differentiate the important from the trivial.
I will decide which path to follow, make a conscious choice rather than stumbling blindly on my way.
The demands of others, with their own agendas pour in upon me until I can no longer remember my own priorities, can no longer find the time to deal with my own needs.
I will set these demands aside, assert myself once more, find my own identity which has become buried under the roles that are thrust upon me by others.

I will re-engage with souls that are important to me, those who lift my spirit, make no demands upon me, who love me for who I am, not what I can do for them.
I will spend time in the places Spirit provides when I need to escape from a world that troubles me, engage with the land, the sea, the elements.
I will draw energy from these places and leave them renewed and serene.

I will take care of my own physical needs to keep the vehicle in which I travel performing at its best.
I will nourish it the best I can and not pollute it with toxins that I pretend to myself I need.
I will treat it with respect and it will carry me forward.
I will take time just to breathe.
I will.

It's Complicated

Why do human beings make life so complicated?

You tie yourselves up in knots and then have to seek out the simple things to heal the damage done by your complications.

You pull away from us, away from the place from whence you came.

You forget us while you live your complicated existence.
But then you must return to us, to a simpler time, a simpler existence to heal the damage you have done.

We provide these places for you and we welcome you back to them with open arms and open hearts.

You dwell with us for a while but then you insist on returning to your complicated ways.

You could be with us always...refusing to engage with the complicated rules that you set for yourselves.

This energy is always available yet you do not seek it as often as you need to....even those of you that claim to work as healers.

Why do you do this?

Draw back inside yourselves often...you should do this at least daily.

Draw away from the complications of your lives.
We can then give you the answers that you seek and the energy that you need to continue.

We are so very close to you but we need you to take that tiny step back so you may find us again.

Let this become a habit, a ritual that you will follow for the rest of your days.

You do not need to cope with the trials of your lives alone.
There are no extra points scored for behaving this way.

The animal kingdom knows this and would never behave as you do.

You think you do not need us in your life and indeed you may choose to live this way.

But why on earth would you?

Live and Let Live

We should not complicate other people's lives.
Their journey will hold enough challenges without our adding unnecessarily to their burden.

We should not seek to make difficulties out of spite, or for revenge or because we enjoy the power of watching another struggle.

If someone has hurt us then allow karma to achieve its outcome in the fullness of time.

It is not for you to bring pressure to bear upon them to achieve your own ends.

Follow your own path, stay focused upon it, do not be distracted from making your own progress by interfering with the progress of others.

Man of Many Words

Plentiful are the words of others.
They talk so much surely there can be nothing left for them to say?

We tire of the sound of their voices, long for them to fall silent.
When the silence comes it feels like a void that should be filled.
Enjoy it while it lasts, they will soon speak again.
Their rhetoric divides nations that should be united, turns friends into enemies, neighbours into strangers, builds walls between souls that should live in harmony in a world that is bountiful.
Sufficient for all if only it is shared equally.
But you must be prepared to work for your share, do not expect charity.
That should be saved only for those who cannot provide for themselves.
Not those who will not.

Look to your leaders to lead you out of darkness.
Support them in their endeavours for they are the leaders you chose.

Theirs is not any easy task.
They have much to learn.

Natural Progression

Go forth into the wilderness.
Seek out its simplicity.
Leave the complicated world in which you live for a while and seek out solitude in the world of nature.

Seek out green fields, the shade of trees, the heights of mountains and the depths of valleys.

Seek out the movement of the sea, use its calming ebb and flow to calm your troubled mind and soothe your soul.
Such simplicity, but it brings great relief from the trials and tribulations of your life.

Time to think, to consider your direction, to seek ways to improve your lot and find your path forwards.

You are so troubled by the haste and busyness of your world that you take no time to consider these things.
But these are the very things that you <u>must</u> do if you are to make progress.

Time spent in nature is never wasted.
Do not feel guilty for taking time out of your day to enjoy its wonders.

It will bring more to you than you could have imagined.
Then you can proceed with your life, renewed and healed.

New Arrivals

You are standing in a world that you have created.
You can be who you want to be.
You can draw those to you who will help you on your journey.
If a new soul appears before you, take note of their arrival.
Seek out the knowledge you should from them.
Give them the knowledge they seek from you.
You should enrich each other's lives.
The soul that arrives may not seem as if they bring a benefit to your existence.
They may bring with them pain and suffering.
They may arouse within you emotions which you do not wish to feel, which you did not seek.
You should embrace these emotions wholeheartedly.
Do not turn away from the opportunity to feel new things, learn new lessons.
Face them with courage and the lesson will soon be done.
Learn once.
Learn well.
Move on.

Make Peace

You have the right to take offence, but I have the right to give it.
You do not have the right to live free of other people's opinions.
There are those who make being offended their life's work.
They take offence at the slightest thing, when none was intended.
They seek out injustice against themselves where none exists.
They like to feel hard done by, that life has treated them unfairly.
But the truth is that none of us deserves an easy ride with a happy ending.
If you think that is why you are here then you have missed the point of your journey.
A life wasted with nothing learned, no spiritual growth achieved.
Look around you.
Look at those who tread the hardest road.
Those for whom life contains so many trials.
Watch them rise above their pain and suffering.
Watch as they still find time to help others despite needing help themselves.
Do they smile often; do they appreciate the smallest blessing?
Are they well loved by those around them?
Are they tolerant of the misdemeanours of others?
Do they forgive easily?

These are the qualities that will bring peace into your heart.
Take an interest in the trials of others and your own will seem less.
You will feel less hard done by if you can see how hard done by others are.
You will feel less offended if you try to see another's point of view.
Do not allow yourself to take offence when none was intended.
Gently guide others along the same path and you will bring peace.

Possessions

You have become trapped by your possessions.
Held in a state where you spend all your time taking care of them.
Repairing them, cleaning them, organising them, protecting them.
What a waste of your life.
Such time as could be spent with loved ones.
Such time could be spent in nature.
Such time could be spent servicing your soul, not servicing your chattels.
For us, possessions were an encumbrance.
Something to carry as we travelled.
Something to protect from attack.
So much easier if we had little, to keep that which we had.
You would do well to learn from this.
Do not hoard that which serves no purpose.
Only seek that which you need, not that which you desire to hold.

Note from Author: Channelled in circle 20th March 2017 from Native American Spirit

Puzzles

The challenges that are sent to perplex you can be the most rewarding to solve.
Like a puzzle that frustrates you but at the same time cannot be set aside.
You keep returning to it time and again as your mind refuses to admit defeat.
Refuses to accept that it might be insoluble.
So it is with life.
See each challenge as a game; keep returning to it until the pennies drop.
Like a maze where you have to keep retracing your steps but making some progress each time.
You cannot expect to solve every challenge at your first attempt. Where would be the fun in that?

Life is like a jigsaw, so many possibilities for all the pieces, so many permutations.
But it will only produce the final image when all are assembled in the right order.
The challenge is to complete the picture without losing any of the pieces.
This would leave holes that can never be filled.
Like the gaps in our lives left by those we have lost.
We have seen the pieces, we know they were there.
But they have slipped from our grasp and remain but a memory.
We can imagine them there, still a part of our whole.
Invisible to others but with us always.
Completing our picture.

One of Many, Part of One

Engage every fibre of your being on your journey here.
Do not drift through life, paying scant attention to the world around you.
Let your eyes focus on your reality, on the gifts and visions that we put before you.
The sky, the sunsets, the stars, the art that nature provides for the gallery of your mind.
Remember these visions well, carry them with you as you journey onwards.

Listen to the sounds that surround you, the wind, the rain, the sea.
The music of the earth that will accompany the journey of your soul.
Engage your other senses, touch, taste and smell.
Focus on embracing all aspects of the life before you.
Use the senses with which you are blessed to heighten your experience of this world.
Ground yourself upon this earth plane as you settle in to enjoy the ride.

Engage too with the feelings and emotions that we place over you.
Do not fear their intensity; use them to help you choose your direction.
Remove yourself from that which disgusts you; do not tolerate its presence.
Be drawn to that which evokes love in you but only if you are loved in return.
Use your response to these emotions to change your world.
When you leave this place it should be the better for you having been here.

Listen too sometimes, to the silence that will empty your head of earthly troubles.
Embrace too, the darkness for it is then that you will feel us draw close to you.
Feel again the touch of Spirit; join again with the oneness of all things.
That you may also remember from whence you came, that you are part of a whole.
That you are never alone.

Optimism Versus Pessimism

An optimist can take the most tragic aspects of life and find something positive in them.
They will find positive lessons in the most negative of situations.
As a result of their optimism they will grow and develop.
They will cope better with life's traumas than a pessimist because they will refuse to see only a negative situation.
They are the ones who will say "things could be worse" when they clearly couldn't be.
They are the ones who will find something to smile at in the saddest of situations.
They are the ones who will feel lucky when they have lost everything.
They are the ones who will feel blessed when others feel bereft.
They will focus on what they have, not what they have not.
They will celebrate what they did, not mourn what they did not.
They will try again when they fail to succeed the first time.
They will find pleasure in the smallest of things, savour every moment of what life has to offer.
The pessimist on the other hand can take the shine from the most special moments that life can provide.
They refuse to learn from the lessons life brings.
Nothing is ever their fault; they will give up at the first hurdle.
They fail to grow, fail to develop to their true potential, while at the same time attempting to suck all around them into their own depressing abyss.

Within most of us exists elements of both the pessimist and the optimist.
How can we feed the optimist while starving the pessimist?
Gratitude will feed the optimist within us.
If we spend a while every day counting our blessings.
Focus on all that is positive in our lives.
If we seek pleasure in the small things even on the darkest of days.
Look for the beauty in our surroundings.
Appreciate the taste of good food.
The sounds of good music and of nature.
The aroma of sweet perfumes.
The warmth of the sun upon our skin.
Take the best that our senses bring to us and hold fast to it.
Starve the pessimist within us by walking away from conflict.
Refuse to be drawn into negative situations.
Talk up, not down.
Close out the pessimism in others around us.
Refuse to acknowledge it.
Tell them to count their blessings too.
Lead by example and others will follow.
May you lift the spirit of all those you encounter on your earthly path.

Wishful Thinking

Wishful thinking paves the way
For wishes to come true,
If you dwell on your wishes,
You will draw your needs to you.
If you are never hopeful
That you'll achieve your life's desires,
Then you'll never see fulfilment
Of the things to which you aspire.
So don't deny your hopes and dreams,
Don't feel you're undeserving,
Your wants and needs have value,
Just as much as those you're serving.
You put other's needs before your own,
And noble though that seems,
You did not come here to serve others
Don't forget your hopes and dreams!

Rise Above

To be kind to someone you have no respect for is difficult but not impossible.
Your humanity should prevail over your emotions.
Set aside your difficulties with them.
Act as you would towards a wounded animal.
It is deserving of your compassion and your desire to end its suffering.
Even souls with no moral compass are deserving of compassion.
You must rise above your emotions, dwell in a higher state.
Then you will know that you take the right path, not a path based on anger or spite.
They still have lessons left to learn.
By acting with compassion you will open them up to a world they do not inhabit.
Show them a way forward based not on fear and jealousy but trust and love.
Show them that there is a better way.
Make sure that you always live by your own high standards however difficult the souls that you encounter on your path.
You should treat them all equally, all kindly.
Then you will know peace of mind.

Past Life Expression

Holistically is how we should think of ourselves, One being, complete in itself, wholly together.

We separate ourselves into mind, body, spirit.
Treat each part in isolation.
We see our body sometimes as a list of ailments.
Not connected, but separate.

We cannot see the lines that join the dots,
join our problems together, link them to each other.
Our physical issues are linked to experiences that have gone before.
Our unfinished business.

Until we deal with these issues our ailments will continue to plague us.
We need to look within for the answers.
We seek cures from those who do not really have our well-being at heart.

There are many who only seek to make money from our misfortunes.
They look at each physical issue in isolation.
Trying to cure a symptom when they should seek its cause.

Many of our ailments are the results of our behaviour in this life.
But some may link into lives from before.
We carry our history forward.

It shapes who we become.

We must address our previous sufferings to release our sufferings in this life.

Go back into our past, seek the knowledge from within.
Go safely; be supported in your travels.
Do not journey alone.

To re-experience traumas past may not be a pleasant experience.

The emotions that may surface may bring fear.
Be prepared that you are not just a spectator.

You will feel the emotions of the events you see.
Understand how these events influence your present life.

Release the traumas that have gone before.

Same Difference

If you cut me do I not bleed, am I not the same as you beneath this skin?
Yet you hate me, without even knowing me.
You are so sure that I am wrong, yet you have never spoken to me.
So sure that I commit sin, yet you do not know my actions.
You judge me, yet you do not think it appropriate that I should judge you.
I have my freedom, but it was hard fought for by my ancestors.
You think I would give it up so easily, succumb to your rules, your standards?
You are no more right than I am, we choose different pathways
But who is to say which of us is right?
I have my preferences; you have yours, different ideals, different beliefs.
So many different ways of life upon this planet, both in the past and present.
Probably in the future too as history repeats itself over and again.
Could we not just agree to differ, leave each other to our own beliefs?
Why do you feel the need to impose your beliefs upon me?
Why do you not trust me to make my own decisions?
I have the same abilities to think as you, the same intelligence.
I can work things out for myself; I do not need your intolerance.
You should listen to the voice within, not the voices of others.
The answers lie within you, seek them out and you will understand all things.
Comprehend that we are all linked to the same source.
We are all the same beneath this skin.
But we should respect our chosen differences.

Signs of the Times

We are shown what we need to see,
told what we need to hear.
The guidance comes, whether we ask for it or not.

We can choose to ignore it, either deliberately or simply because we are not looking for it.
In our isolation we refuse to accept the help that is available to us.

We struggle when there is no need.
We suffer when we could be healed.
We starve when we could receive sustenance.

See the signs for what they are and stop ignoring them.
Seek them out and accept what is freely offered.

Precious Gifts

We all have gifts that we can share with others, whether we realise it or not.

It is in sharing these gifts that we feel part of the whole.
Our creativity links us with others.

When we create, be it drawing, writing, singing, sewing, knitting or baking and then share our creations with others we have given a part of ourselves to someone else.

Something to remember us by, to connect us with a loved one or a complete stranger.

We all have a memory of something that someone made and gave to us.

Even something as simple as the picture a child brings home from school.

These things become prize possessions or precious memories.
Far more so than something somebody bought us.

It is a little piece of them for us to keep, sometimes long after we have been parted from them.

Every time we look at it, it brings them close again.

That need to create is so strong within us that we are unfulfilled without it.
It matters not how small our creations are, a baked cake that is shared or a piece of knitting given away.

What matters is that we have shared our gifts and brought joy to others.

So it is with spiritual gifts.

If we have the ability to connect with Spirit we should do so.
We should have the confidence to share our results.
Spirit sends these messages to bring comfort, clarity and to remove the fear of what is to come.

Sometimes these messages will be some of the most important words that a soul will hear in their lifetime.
They should be shared, and widely, that we may illuminate the path for others.

Stairway to Heaven

How many stairs you have to climb.
Just when you think you are done for a while there appears yet another flight, your pause merely a breather as if upon a landing.
A chance to get your breath back then off you go again.

I am sorry if your burdens get heavier the further you climb.
You should try putting some down.
Setting them aside as tasks completed that need not be taken up again.
You can revisit them, but why would you?
You have worked hard to complete them once; there is no need to repeat a step once it has been climbed.

You can go down as well as up but there is no need to descend.
No need to revisit past mistakes, past misdemeanours.
You have learned those lessons, put them from your mind and forgive yourself for your failures.

All will become victories before your time is done.

The Gardeners

That we will find ways to contact you is not in doubt.
The only doubt is in whether you will see the signs for what they are.

You brush things off as coincidences or your imagination.
You steadfastly refuse to believe that we would send a message just for you.
How much evidence do you need that you are not alone?
From the lights that flicker to the songs that you hear with lyrics that could only be for you.
Pay heed to these things and you will find the comfort that you need.
The courage to step forward with us right beside you.

We will put people in front of you that you can cling on to.
Do not be afraid to lean on them, it is why they are there.
Once you have reached your goal you can repay their kindness.
Do for them what they have done for you.

You are like a beanstalk, unsupported you will never climb far from the ground.
You will waver and fall when the wind blows as you do not have the strength to stand alone.
Like a gardener we will provide support to enable you to blossom and reach great heights.

But you must choose to use it.

The Gift of Sleep

The gift of sleep eludes me so,
It dangles before me just beyond my reach.
I am so close but the more I stretch out towards it, the further it retreats.

I swear it laughs at me as I grope blindly for it in the dark.
So near yet so far away.
How many hours must we play this game tonight?
I try to trick it into submission.
I feign indifference; pretend I do not seek it at all.

I rise for a while, then sneak back into my bed when I think it is not looking.
I pray it does not notice me slide between the covers.
Can I sneak up on it, catch it unawares?
Claim it for my own before it eludes me once again?
Wrap my weary body in its soft embrace?

I feel like a child, trying to catch a snowflake.
As soon as it touches my skin it is gone, melted away by the warmth of me.

Maybe if I read awhile sleep will creep up behind me?
I will pretend to be so absorbed in the words that I no longer seek its solace.
Sleep will peek over my shoulder to see what it is missing.
I will let it rest upon the page before I slam the book shut.
Trap it between the pages before it can escape again.
I have tried this before, it is rarely a success.

Like a fly it evades capture again and again.
I chase it around the room but it disappears into the dark.
My mind it needs to rest, it screams for respite from the trials of the day.

My worries play over and over in my head like a loop of film.
With each repeat they grow bigger until I have no hope of hiding from them.

Sleep would bring escape, I could travel with the angels,
Dream the answers that I need, for they would surely bring them to me.

Before I know, the night is gone and it is time to rise.
I must resume my earthly duties, tired and confused.

Until the night time, when the game begins again.

Note from Author: For Colin Fuller, our Church President in Spirit

The Master

Master of souls, of all eternity.
Leading the way out of the darkness and into a world of light.
The darkness must come first, for without the darkness who would appreciate the light?

Master of love, of all emotions.
All must be felt, one after another, until the only emotion remaining is love.
The others must be seen for what they are.
False masters who will lead you down the wrong paths until eventually you learn that the only way forward is in love.

Master of all time and space, infinite in all directions, into the past and into the future.
Join with me and become masters of your own destiny.

The Road to Hell

So close to being who we want to be, what holds us back from being that person?

We know how we want to behave and in our head we are that person but our actions and words betray our aims time and again.

Others see a side of us we would prefer to hide, would prefer did not exist.
But if it is in us how can we change it?
We try to bury it, to deny it but it is part of who we are.
We can choose not to express it.
To look at that part of us and not let it control us or our actions.

We must keep bringing ourselves back to our intent.

If we do not intend to hurt others then we must ensure that our emotions do not override our intentions.
If we do not intend to commit evil acts then we must ensure that our actions do not override our intentions.
If we intend to progress in this world then we must ensure that our actions override our inertia.
If we intend to attract love then we must ensure that we give love.

Intent is but a starting point.

Only actions will make our intentions reality.

The Helpers

The Angels are with you always, but it is your choice whether you call upon them.
They are helpers and guides, supporters and facilitators of your journey.
You can visualise them however you choose, they have no form.
They will appear to you in a way that reassures you, comforts you and leaves no doubt that you are supported in your endeavours.
You may ask for their assistance whenever you are troubled, lost or afraid.
They will bring you upliftment, often in the simplest of ways.
They will bring light into your darkness, music into your silence, warmth into your cold existence.
They will put signs before you to reassure you that you follow the right path.
How will you recognise these signs for what they are and not just the trivia of the world around you?
The simple answer is that if you wonder if something is a sign, then it is a sign.
If the thought enters your head that you are being helped and guided then you are being helped and guided.
You may take what you wish from the signs or you may choose to ignore them.
We will keep putting them before you until realisation eventually dawns.
Angels are patient beings and once you realise their assistance is available to you your path will become a whole lot easier.
Then you will seek the signs and follow them, trusting their significance as a bird trusts the signs we place before it on its migratory path.

Make Time

Make time for yourself, make time for your needs,
Stop falling for those souls who make your heart bleed,
They sap all your strength, take away the resolve,
That you need for your issues and problems to solve.
Step away from the takers and fakers and lies,
Step away from the gossips, the stirrers and spies,
Be true to yourself, you know what you need,
To grow and develop YOUR soul you must feed.
Give guidance to those who are struggling for sure,
But don't do their tasks for them when they come back for more,
Make some space in your life for a new role for you,
It may be quite simple, look around for a clue.
At the back of your mind is a long desired dream,
Making it reality is not as hard as it seems,
Put a thought to the angels, ask for help just for you,
If you ask, you will get, and your dreams will come true.

The Season of Pointless Gifts

To preserve your world you must step forward and lead by example.
Do it now.
Do not say "We should do this" or "We should do that".
Just do it.
Then it will become the norm.
You should discourage materialism for it serves no purpose.
Your season of pointless gifts has come upon you.
You should put careful thought into the gifts that you give or desire.
Let charity benefit from your finances.
Lead by example and let the gifts you ask for benefit others.
Ask for donations to charity in your name.
This will preserve the Earth's resources.
You have allowed this festival to become so materialistic.
The leader of men whose birth you celebrate would not desire this in his name.
This man desired charity, his life was charity, his work was charity.
You have turned this festival into a monstrosity.
Yet the love is still there for friends and family.
Use this festival to make contact with them, he would approve of this.
Seek out those you love and spend time together.
Let the gifts you exchange be charitable and purposeful not just material.
That is the way forward.

Ignorance is Not Bliss

You must not lower yourself to the level of others.
Hold fast to your values, your own truths.
Do not fear to stand by your beliefs.
Do not allow them to be diluted by the ignorant.
It is your job to educate these souls.
Lead them out of their darkness and into your light.
Do not let bigotry go unchallenged.
It is what others did before you and led to genocide.
Do not fear to be the first to raise a voice against it.
Others will follow your lead.
The voice of reason must be heard above the voice of ignorance.
Do not allow yourself to be dragged into shouted arguments.
Speak clearly, repeat yourself as often as it takes to be heard.
Those who shout will lose their voice eventually.
Let the voice of reason continue long after the shouting has ceased.
Then you will be heard.

The Source

We are a product of our ancestors, we carry their genes, exhibit their traits.
But the spirit that dwells within comes with no traits, no distinguishing characteristics, no habits.
It is pure energy, travelling away from source but still connected to a greater consciousness.

We can link back in to this greater consciousness of which we are all a part.
When we link we leave behind the products of our genes and join again to our source.
We step back from our body and go within ourselves to find our source again.

We can link to any part of the source.
We can be shown that which we need to assist our journey on the earth plane.
We will only be allowed to remember that which will not interfere with our journey here.
The rest must remain hidden inside until we return to the source.

Our genes were chosen to shape our behaviour, our challenges, our appearance.
They will colour our journey, determine our progress, define us whilst we are here.
We do not take them with us when we leave this plane.
They do not define the source.
The source exhibits no emotions, carries no anger, no jealousy, no hate, no despair.

We leave these emotions behind and take only the lessons learned from engaging with them.
When we return it is to calm, to peace, to tranquillity as we reconnect to source.
What is the role of love in this process?
Is it an emotion that is also left behind?
Love is a gift from source.
It is sent to remind us where we have come from.

When we return to source we return to the source of love.
It is not what defines us on the earth plane.
It is what defines the source.

To the Bitter End?

Sometimes we are so sure of our path in life that we follow it blindly, stumbling over or veering round the obstacles in our way that are clearly trying to tell us we are going in the wrong direction.

It is true that life is not meant to be easy.
There will be obstacles to test our mettle.
There will be tests of our perseverance, to ensure that our rewards have been earned.

But there will be times when we are simply going the wrong way.

Times when our actions will not cause us to fulfil our destiny.
At what point should we give up and take another path?
How can we tell what is a test of our perseverance and what is a sign to turn back?

That Spirit sends these signs is not in doubt.
Petty frustrations that prevent our forward movement or prevent us finishing a task.
Tools that break, domestic crises that delay progress towards our heart's desires.

Once, twice, thrice these may be tests of endurance.
But repeated petty frustrations should cause us to step back and examine our choices.

Could there be another way for us?
Another road, another opportunity that our delays have given us time to see.

We should not doggedly follow a path that does not serve our purpose.
Just because we have spent a long time and a great deal of effort making a mistake that does not mean we have to continue with it until the bitter end.
See the petty frustrations for the signs that they are and ask yourself the question...

"Is this the right path or is there another way for me?"

A Compromising Situation

Manipulation is the name of the game if you want to get your way,
Make others think it is their idea and your plans will get their say.
There are always two sides to dilemmas and to change others' minds will take tact,
But if you bury your head and say nothing, you'll get nowhere and that's just a fact.
Shouting your views achieves nothing; you must keep your cool to succeed,
Violence is also not helpful, when you're trying to get what you need.
If your views are truly the right ones, then you should have nothing to fear,
But you must also listen to others, even if you'd prefer not to hear.
Know that deep down inside is a spirit, that knows what is right and is wrong,
You must listen to yours just as others, can be persuaded to hear spirit's song.
Lay out the facts for inspection; think through the options in view,
Think 'outside the box' if you must, 'cause I'm told that's what clever people do.
Be fair in your judgments and actions; let others folks too, have their say,
It may be that you need to compromise, rather than just try to get your own way!

A Little Illumination

Many more lights they are needed,
Many more lights need to mark,
The road along which some folk travel,
To help lead them out of the dark.
Some folk spend their whole life in darkness,
They can't see the path they must take,
Don't realise just how much they're missing,
Can't see the mistakes that they make.
They don't learn to progress from their failures,
Make the same mistakes over again,
Though they may be here for a long time,
They do so much for so little gain.
How can we provide illumination,
To those who struggle so hard just to see?
We know that the light's all around us,
And will light up our pathway for free.
It strengthens and lifts us beyond life,
Takes us to worlds hidden to some,
They would be so welcome to join us,
And we'd be so glad if they'd come!

Ascends Another Hero

You don't need to do much to be important,
You can make a difference in such simple ways.
You don't need to seek out fame and fortune,
You can be a hero every day.
There is no need for fast cars and big houses,
To make your mark upon the world you know,
To bring meaning to your life always remember,
That for rewards you always reap just what you sow.
'And not let us be weary in well doing:
For in due season will shall reap, if we faint not.'
We should look outwards, to the needs of others,
Looking inwards won't make us happy with our lot,
In helping others we will find the satisfaction,
Of knowing that a job has been well done,
In turn, we will find, we are respected,
And if we need help be sure someone will come.
We will be remembered for what we did for others,
Not for all the times we saw fit not to act,
So when the time comes for our passing,
We will take with us all the love the selfish lack.

Note from Author: For Mike. One of life's heroes.

Includes quote from King James Bible: Galatians 6:9

Thinking Time

No voice is needed for communication to take place.
We come mind to mind, soul to soul.
We are with you all the time.

We put ideas into your minds to make you move on.
Your light bulb moments come from us to push you along your path.

If you relax and let us in we can give you so much more.
Do not deny us.
You will run with us.
You will walk alone.

Give us the time we need to penetrate your barriers.
Let us into your busy world.
Take time to think.

It will allow us to bring so much to you.

We would love to ease your path.

But you must let us in.

Ask the Angels

Manifesting your heart's desires is not an easy task,
But rest assured it's easier if you have the nerve to ask.
Put your thoughts into the ether to let the angels know,
That you need a little help to get the things that you want so.
It's not like asking Santa for a list of material things,
The possessions you desire cannot be carried on angel's wings.
But if you need help with your worst fears they are the place to go,
To help you to overcome the things that scare you so.
If it's jealousy that troubles you that you don't want to feel,
Ask them to lift it from you, let it go so you can heal.
Such destructive emotions can only bring you harm,
Banish forever, the green-eyed monster's charm.
If anger rules your life, ask the angels for advice,
On how to quell the rage within before you pay the price,
You will do things that you'll regret in the heat of anger's fire,
Ask the angels to send some love to bring the calm that you desire.
When sadness overtakes you due to things you can't control,
Give your worries to the angels before depression takes a hold,
Put the word up to them that you need help with your lot,
Say a little prayer for answers to ease the troubles that you've got.
The angels will put before you all the things you need,
To change path you travel if you would but take heed.
Try not to miss the signs or push away the ones they send,
To help you reach your goals and get the life that you intend.

The Land

The land is the place to be.
It soothes the soul like no city ever can.
It is where you are from and where you belong.
You should return often.
It will complete you.

The energy you gain will fortify you; build you up so you can proceed.
Listen to its sounds.
Look at its colours.
Feel its strength.

It will fulfil your every need.
Let it lead you by the hand into a world of wonderment, away from the trials of your day.

Then you may return to your world renewed and strengthened, to continue on your path.

Believe in Yourself

The secret of success is confidence, in all we try to do,
If we do not believe we will succeed, then failure will creep through.
It must not be an option, we must just close it out,
That we'll succeed in our endeavours, must never be in doubt.
Trust in your ability, be guided on your path,
Don't let fear of failure undermine all your hard graft.
You are as worthy as the next of triumph in your chosen field,
But you must believe in your ability or else your fate is sealed.
There will be others all around you, who shout how good they are,
And those who shout the loudest, will seem the brightest star.
They will walk upon the dreams of those who hold themselves in check,
And they will not care as they climb up how many dreams they wreck.
All for one and one for all does not work in this world,
It's more like every man for himself, as through life we are hurled.
Robert the Bruce sussed it all out as the spider worked in vain,
If at first you don't succeed, then try, try, try again!

Changing Direction

We are so busy doing, as we rush through life head first,
We take on so much information, it's a wonder we don't burst.
We should take time to slow it down, to step back from the brink,
We should make space inside our heads to give us time to think.
We cannot plan our future if we don't look to the fore,
We'll just keep plodding on, doing what we did before.
We'll work ourselves into the ground, toiling every day,
Before we know it, life is done and in our grave we lay.
So look at what you're doing, are you where you want to be?
Are you with the ones that inspire you, fulfil you spiritually?
You can change the pathway, find another one to tread,
If you look inside, you'll find the answers in your head.
Listen to the voices, don't try to block them out,
Don't ignore the signals, they are sent to help you out.
Coincidences don't exist, they're all part of the plan,
Things happen for a reason, that's all you need to understand!

Bury the Victor in You

Churlish behaviour is no help at all,
It aggravates others, drives them up the wall,
Being pedantic will irritate too,
You need to acknowledge others' points of view.
You're not always right; you must learn to see,
That there is more than just one way to be.
We all have a choice of how we want to live,
It's not your place to judge, you must learn how to give.
You won't want to hear the words on this page,
In fact they are likely to put you in a rage,
It is easy to criticise, it is the lazy man's way,
To make conversation when you've nothing to say,
But it soon becomes habit and before very long,
It is all that you do and I'm afraid that's just wrong,
You must seek out the positive in the people you know,
They are doing their best to help their spirit grow.
We all have our problems, no one's perfect you see,
So cut them some slack, just leave them be.
Let them make their mistakes, that's how they will learn,
Support their endeavours, each task in its turn,
Encourage and mentor, don't just give critique,
Accept that each one of us is truly unique,
Help others play to their strengths if you can,
It will make you a humbler and more tolerant man,
If you support others in their trials you will find,
That you've plenty to say and your words will be kind.

Animal Magic

The start of something new brings excitement, motivation and energy.
The start of a new day brings hope that today may bring great things.
The disappointments of yesterday fade into the past as we face the world anew.
The generation of a new life through the miracle of birth brings with it love.
It arouses emotions and instincts in us that drive us to protect the new arrival.
It motivates us to do our very best to support it.
The birth of an animal produces the same instincts in us as the birth of a baby.
With this new arrival comes much responsibility as we seek to keep it safe.
The love and companionship that comes with it will lift our spirit.
It will make us feel needed, make us feel wanted, banish loneliness.
Whatever we give to them will return to us many times over.
They will not argue with us, will not betray us, will not play games with our emotions.
They will show us loyalty and love in return for the care that we give them.
They will heal the wounds that life inflicts upon us and make us feel whole again.
They will give us purpose if before we could find none.
They accept us for who we are and do not try to change us.
They come into our lives as gifts from Spirit to enrich our lives and share our journey.

Choices

There are no right answers so we are often told,
Just decisions we can live with as our paths through life unfold.
You can only make the choice that feels right on the day,
You cannot foresee the future to see how things will play.
It's no good looking back at life and feeling just regret,
You did the best you could and that you should not forget.
When making a decision listen to your inner voice,
The lesser of two evils is sometimes the only choice.

You can weigh up pros and cons and write them all out in a list,
But the answer to your dilemma may still be hidden in the mist.
Your list may show that all the cons are outweighed by the pros,
But something may still hold you back, why is that do you suppose?
Trust the instinct deep inside you, it is there to give a clue,
When everyone around is giving different points of view,
You can ask too many people what they would do in your shoes,
But you're the one that's wearing them so don't let them confuse.

The choice you make may provoke transformations in your world,
And change can bring fear with it as the future is unfurled.
Fear of the unknown can cause us to paralyse,
'Better the devil you know' may sound like good advice,
But when inertia stops progression and our drive for life has gone,
Sometimes a leap of faith is what is needed to move on.
There will be clues along the way to tell us which way we should leap,
We should pay particular attention to the ones when we're asleep.

Our dreams may give the link to guidance from above
When we've ground to a halt and need a little shove,
Or a series of coincidences may put chances in our way,
Just trust that these were all deliberate as Spirit has its say.
Don't ignore the signs you're sent to guide you on your path,
Walk away from things that make you cry, chase those that make you laugh,
You can be sure that doing nothing will not change the status quo,
So make a choice and you will be amazed how far you go!

Cosmic Ordering

What shall I do? Where shall I go?
So many choices confuse me so.
I could carry on doing what I do,
But then I'd never do anything new.
Never move ahead, never learn new things,
While I sit and wait to see what life brings.
But I want control, want to be in charge
Of my fate, my destiny, my world at large.
I must put out the thoughts of my hopes and my schemes,
So that they will return to me and fulfil my dreams.
I can ask for some guidance as I go along,
Seek help from the heavens when things all go wrong.
I don't need to struggle when alone and afraid,
I can just ask for help when my plans get waylaid.
The route to my goal, it may twist, it may turn,
But each time it wavers, a lesson I learn.
That I will still get there, I must never doubt,
I must never forget what my journey's about.
Hold fast to my dreams and my hopes and desires,
Let the universe bring me all my soul requires.

Death's Door

We are all at Death's door, my dear,
One wrong move and we're out of here.
So full of life, so close to death,
Only separated by one last breath.
One heartbeat away, from being cold and grey,
So near, yet so far away.

What keeps us here, alive and kicking?
Our breath still warm, our heart still ticking.
Our hold on life is fragile, so
It would be easy to let go.
Just slip away, at close of play,
Choose not to fight another day.

Our ties to life can be so strong,
The loves we have, for which we long
Will hold us here, to life we bond,
With no desire to go beyond.
They bind us tight, from day to night,
We cling to life with all our might.

But time must pass, we age and fade,
We look back on the life we made.
The loves we had, the loves we lost,
The scars left as from life they crossed.
Our hold grows weak, our loves we seek,
And round Death's door we bravely peek.

Does Your Inside Match Your Outside?

Does your inside match your outside? Do you put on a brave face?
Before you leave the house do you paint a smile in place?
Do you hide all your troubles behind a stuck on mask?
Do you just say "I'm fine" if ever someone asks?
How many times have you dodged the chance to tell friends how you feel?
When deep inside there is a wound you think will never heal.
You don't want to bother folk, you think that they won't care,
You think no-one likes a whinger so your troubles you won't share.

You've a shoulder others cry on, your friendship it is true,
The friends that you won't bother, will soon offload on you.
They think you've all the answers to all their fears and woes,
They trust you with their secrets, they share their highs and lows.
Your discretion it is legend, your lips stay tightly sealed,
As they heap their troubles on you so their worries can be healed.
You would never turn someone away who needs to bend your ear,
You have the gift of counselling to help to quell their fear.

But don't forget your own needs, don't bury them inside,
Your troubles should be dealt with, there is no need to hide.
Don't lock them in a box and throw away the key,
You will have to take them out and look at them eventually.
Your friends may just surprise you, with the answers that you need,
That a trouble shared is halved is very true indeed.
Your friends think you're invincible but you know that's not true,
Let your inside match your outside, and they will help you too!

Don't Forget Me

Trapped in a world that I can't remember,
Life now an illness no-one else can forget,
Just a shadow of me remains in my body,
The me you see now is not the me that you met.
My soul still intact in the wreck of my body,
Can be seen in my eyes if you gaze within,
While I gaze out on a world, unfamiliar,
Recognising no one, in a game I can't win.
You keep trying to reach me but I'm not replying,
You try to remind me who I was before,
When we were both young and in love with each other,
But I am no longer that girl anymore.
She spends her time outside of this body,
She visits the angels in a realm far away,
She comes and she goes now, just as she pleases,
She follows you home at the end of the day.
Don't worry about her; she's free now and happy,
But she sees you shed tears for the girl that you've lost,
You are already mourning the loss of my spirit,
While the care of my body still comes at great cost.
Make some time for yourself now while you are still able,
Don't worry about this body that refuses to die,
Don't feel guilty for not coming each day to see me,
My spirit goes with you so let your tears dry.
Travel to the places that we went to together,
Visit the loved ones and the friends that remain,
I will be by your side now and forever,
So let us go travelling together again.

Do As You Would Be Done By

Be kind to others we are always told,
Be kind to the young, be kind to the old.
Be kind to animals, the fish and the birds,
Be kind to the ignorant, be kind to the nerds.
Treat everyone as you'd have them treat you,
Try to see everyone's point of view.
Be a friend to those souls less fortunate than you,
Be a help to the helpless, those that haven't a clue.
Be there for your friends in their hour of need,
Be there for your neighbour in thought, word and deed.
And when you've done all these things, for the sake of your health,
Make sure you remember, to take care of yourself!

Enquire Within

Help me make the journey, help me see where my path lies,
Help me to step forward, when fear leaves me paralysed.
Send me guidance I can trust when I can't see which way to go,
Send me clues to all the questions whose answers I don't know.
I know I have free will and I could choose my way myself,
And I could seek out answers from the books upon the shelf.
But that feeling in my gut is what I must come to trust,
When I need some assistance to make choices that I must.

I can study all the pros and cons and weigh them up for days,
Look at problems from all angles and in umpteen different ways,
I can ask my family and my colleagues or even 'phone a friend,
Until my lack of a decision drives them all around the bend.
But I should look inside myself for answers I can't find,
And seek out intuition from inside my own mind.
I should use the tools God gave me, to guide me on my way,
And to help with the decisions with which I'm faced each day.

If in doubt do nothing, is rarely a good choice,
It is the choice of fear which I must not let be my voice,
So next time I am struggling to work out what to do,
I'll try not overthink but let gut instinct see me through.
Whether I am right or whether I am wrong,
I must just keep going forwards; I must not stand still for long,
And if things don't turn out in the end quite the way I'd planned,
I'm sure there'll be a lesson there I need to understand.

Information Overload

The truth is hard to find in this world today.
So much information you are drowning in it.
But what is true and what is fiction?
What is fact and what is opinion?
So difficult to differentiate, it is easy to stop listening.
If you are not hearing the truth then why bother?
You cannot take on board the troubles of the entire planet.
Yet they are put before you on a daily basis for you to worry about.
You are overwhelmed with the world's sadness.
You would love to solve all the world's problems but that is not possible.
Be careful that the overwhelm does not destroy you.
Pay attention to your immediate surroundings, your loved ones and your own issues.
These are the problems to which you should pay heed.
If you have time to spare by all means spread your attention further, but do not spread it so thinly that you have no effect on the outcomes.
Pick your favourite challenges, devote your efforts to these.
For the rest, send out your prayers and leave the angels do your bidding.
Trust that it is all for good reason and let your worries go.
You cannot do it all alone.

Evidence Based Religion

Clever people say there is no God, no life to come.
They think they know it all, but inside they are numb.
They focus on their Earthly life, possessions they collect,
But though their house is full, their heart is empty I suspect.
They do not see the world around them, do not understand their role,
They do not realise they're here for the progress of their soul.
Why does it not puzzle them, the reason they are here?
They plod through every day, through every month, through every year.
Their progress they will measure by accumulated wealth,
They do not see the riches in good friends and in good health.
The challenges they face they do not see as means to learn,
They just see interruptions to how much they can earn.
How can we open up their minds to the reasons they are here?
We can provide the evidence that they refuse to hear.
Some people cannot deal with thoughts that challenge their beliefs,
But the evidence that we can bring can help so much with grief.
When they have lost a loved one their pain is hard to face,
As they believe the one they've lost has left without a trace.
But we know that they still exist, they still will be around,
If we can offer proof then maybe comfort can be found.
When the opportunity presents, we should not fear to give,
Evidence that life goes on and that we're not just here to live!

Fool's Paradise

Life is not fair, there are no rules,
The world's full of wise men, but also of fools.
The wise men keep quiet, they don't feel the need,
To shout from the rooftops, they're wise men indeed.
But sadly, the fools, like to hear their own voice,
And they talk so loudly, the rest have no choice
But to listen to their lunacy, their plans and their schemes,
And all of that drivel that they spout in reams.
They repeat it so often, we start to believe,
That their ideas are valid, but don't be deceived.
Think hard for yourself, make up your own mind,
Look for answers yourself, seek and you will find.
The loud fools seek power, take it from the meek,
But fools don't deserve all the power they seek.
It is time for the wise men to stand up and shout,
Or the fools will take over, of that there's no doubt!

Free Guide with Every Journey

Clever souls these spirits, they support our every move.
They watch us fight our battles and our path they try to smooth.
They try to guide us gently, away from fear and pain,
And if we fail a task they will help us try again.
Our behaviour must frustrate them if we ignore the clues they send,
When we miss all the signals as a hand they try to lend.
It must be like watching telly when our favourite quiz is on,
And we're shouting out the answers when contestants get them wrong.
We bounce up in our seats screaming at the screen,
"How can you be so stupid? You're a disgrace to your team!"
I imagine it is similar for our spirit guides that wait,
Until we finally get the message. They need the patience of a saint!
If your problems keep recurring as you proceed on your way,
Keep an ear out for the guidance, watch for the clues they lay,
They go to so much trouble to help us with every task,
If you cannot see which path to take just say a prayer and ask!

Head Space

Reality sets in when you see how much to do,
Like a rabbit caught in headlights which way to jump is hid from view.
You don't know where to start, which job should be done first,
Inside your head is so much stuff it's a wonder you don't burst.
Panic sets into your mind so no progress is made,
You are paralysed and overwhelmed as through tasks you try to wade.
The golden rule when you are stressed is to step back from the edge,
Take a while to breathe and make yourself a little pledge.
Promise you will take time out to do some things for you,
Life must be worth living not just a pile of jobs to do,
Give yourself some head space every now and then,
When you come back renewed then you can start your tasks again.
Your focus will be stronger and you will achieve much more,
Take one task at a time and you won't panic any more.

Heal Thyself

Let the healing we send lift you out of your misery.
Let the healing we send lift you out of your pain.
It is our gift to ease the path that you travel
When life becomes a little too hard to sustain.
You don't need a healer to bring this gift to you,
Just believe that we'll help every time that you ask,
Draw our energy close as we lift your spirit,
Give you strength to go on and finish your task.

The pills that you pop will not solve all your problems,
They bring with them issues that will challenge you more,
They may mask what you feel but will dull all your senses,
As their side effects you try so hard to ignore.
Let the food we provide be the source of your healing,
Things grown in nature not laboratories clean.
Let your seasoning be the spices the earth grows,
Not the chemicals scientists insert unseen.

Seek the solace of nature to soothe and restore you,
Let peace and tranquillity fill you again.
The animal kingdom has friends who will love you,
Unconditionally, loyally, healing your pain.
Seek the company of souls who will lift and renew you,
Bring laughter and joy to the darkness you see.
Close out the takers who drain and deplete you,
Feel your energy rise as you focus on 'me'.

Take care of the vehicle in which you chose to travel,
To get best performance you must service its needs.
Don't pollute it with toxins that others persuade you,
Will make you feel better. They are poison indeed.
You will find that the answers to all of your troubles,
Can be found if you look in the places you roam.
We will put them before you so please don't ignore them,
We will follow your journey until it's time to come home.

I Have Not Ceased To Be

Do not speak in the past tense,
I have not ceased to be,

If you are still you,
Then I am still me.
Keep saying "she is",
Don't start saying "she was",
Don't question my place in the world now, because
If you are still you,
And I am still me,
Then though you can't see me,
I have not ceased to be.

You can't hear my voice,
You are sure that I've gone,
But if you think I'm no more,
I'm afraid that you're wrong.
I will be for ever,
I have always been,
I, just for a while,
Was the one you have seen.

So think of me always,
Though I could not remain,
I have not ceased to be,
You will find me again.

Infinite Patience

A decision made should be stuck to.
It may take time to achieve.
Don't give up too quickly,
In yourself you must believe.
Sometimes it's just the timing,
So with patience you must wait,
Until the planets come together,
To help fulfil your fate.
If you just consider,
How vast the universe,
How infinite is time and space,
You'll see things could be worse.
If your aims are worth achieving,
Then continue to pursue,
Your hopes and dreams and missions,
Give us time to make them true.
If you consider all the variables,
With which we must contend,
You'll see why you need patience,
When you cannot see the end.
There is work behind the scenes,
You cannot see how hard we try,
To make your mission come together,
We will send help from on high.
Your prayers will soon be answered,
So don't give up on your dream,
You are not in this alone,
You have Spirit on your team.

Inside Information

I have everything I need to know,
To show me which way I should go,
It's not without, it's found within,
It's in my head, inside my skin.
A piece of me, it links into
The universe and all things true.
The knowing's there, if I seek it out,
To tell me what life's all about.
To find the answers that I seek,
Inside my head I need to peek,
To shut the world out I must try,
Spend time alone, my head and I.
For some this is a scary thought,
As solitude they've never sought,
They need company all the while,
To be alone they find a trial.
Our media driven world will fill
The silence when they should be still.
They should embrace some time alone,
Turn off the telly and their 'phone,
Just sit awhile in quiet and dark,
Look inside for that little spark
Of illumination from within,
That will tell you where you should begin.
When all around you falls apart,
And you can't work out where to start,
Be sure to look inside your mind,
If you just seek, then you will find.

Just Ask

The challenges of the day have become hard to bear,
You will not engage with them, feel life's unfair.
Feel alone and despondent, unloved and careworn,
Some days you wish you had never been born.
The people around you can't see how you feel,
You keep it inside, a wound that won't heal.
The face that you show to the world wears a smile,
But the heart that's inside cannot cope with its trials.
You would not let on to those people around,
That you feel overwhelmed, with work you are drowned.
You won't ask for help, you just battle on,
You sit down and cry after everyone's gone.
There is no time for you, your needs go unmet,
There is no chance your troubles you'll ever forget.
There are those who would help if only you'd ask.
Don't feel that you can't ask for help with your task.
No one comes here to do all things alone,
All you need do is just pick up the 'phone.
You'll find someone willing and able for sure,
To help share your burden, they'll never ignore
A true cry for help. They will be there for you,
They will lift and restore you, help you get through.
But they can't read your mind, they think you're ok,
You must open your heart and they'll show you the way.

Just Breathe

No more, no less,
No fuss, no stress,

If life just could
Be always good,
We'd have no cause
To stop and pause,
From life to death,
To just draw breath.
When times are tough,
When life gets rough,
To help relieve,
Take time to breathe,
You know you could,
Inhale the good,
And when you're sad,
Exhale the bad.
Your breath is all
It takes to call,
Close to your side,
Your spirit guide.

Breathe slow and strong,
Breathe deep and long,
Let tension go,
Let spirit flow,
Into your mind,
Let Spirit find
A place where you,
Can escape to,
When life's a mess
and you can't guess,

What you should do,
Seek Spirit's clue.

Keep Your Friends Close…

When your enemies walk amongst you, do not despair,
Do not fear to step outside your door.
When your enemies are invisible, do not fear every shadow,
Be not afraid of what life has in store.
Be brave, be bold, engage with those you fear,
Let them know you, your family, your friends,
Show them love, compassion, friendship,
Do not burn bridges, make amends.

While you see them as your enemy, they see you as theirs,
What can you do to change that state of mind?
It is easy to judge someone you do not know,
But hard to hate someone who's being kind.
Show respect, as you would be respected,
Understand their ways for there are many ways to be,
Not wrong, not right, just different,
Respect their right to choose their way to see.

Ignorance breeds fear, fear brings distrust,
Knowledge brings power, so get to know your rival,
Showing them love disarms distrust,
Listening to their fears aids your survival.
Do not give ground, hold fast to your beliefs,
Welcome debate but do not compromise on your own truths,
Be tolerant, but demand tolerance in return,
Agree to differ, if they cannot offer proof.

Learn to Step Back

A challenge for you, a challenge for me,
One after the other, that's how things should be,
But sometimes they come, so thick and so fast,
That we struggle to cope 'til the crisis has passed.

We think that we can't take on any more,
But the challenges come 'til we can't keep score.
Make sure that you only take on what is yours,
Or you'll get no rest because you never pause.

If the people around you won't deal with their tasks,
Then you must step back when for your help they ask.
If you bail them out then they'll never learn,
And the lesson they've missed will only return.

They cannot move on 'til they get it right,
Don't do it for them 'cause it's not your fight,
So if you are finding you've no time to unwind,

Then let them get on with it, be cruel to be kind!

Learn to Teach, Free Yourself.

Help will be given to all those who ask,
As you struggle each day to complete every task.
They come every way,
Every hour of the day,
Thick and fast from the first to the last.

Just when you think you can't do any more,
Another request will arrive at your door,
"Could you just help me out?
No one else is about",
A demand for help you can't ignore.

We watch as you take on another great pile,
Of some other soul's problems more than once in a while.
You just can't say no,
As they get up and go,
And leave you to sort out their life's trials.

We know that you love to help out and assist,
But you really must learn to step back and resist,
You can still be a guide,
But you must dodge the tide
Of other folk's jobs on your list.

So how do you think you will learn to say no,
To those souls who come to you with their tales of woe?
There is no need to preach,
What you must do is teach,
Help them learn so in turn they will grow.

To keep doing it for them will just hold them back,
You must teach them the skills for the tasks that they lack.
Then send them away,
Give yourself time to play,
Time to do your own thing and relax!

Life is What You Make It

You will remember the days that made you laugh,
You will remember the days that made you cry.
You will remember the days when lives were born,
You will remember the days you said goodbye.

You will forget the days you went to work,
You will forget the toil, the stress, the strain.
You will forget the winters, long and dark,
You will forget the cold, the wind, the rain.

You will remember the things that made you feel,
Strong emotions, good and bad.
They will stay with you 'til your dying day,
Both happy times and days so sad.

The mundane days will fade away,
In retrospect they will merge and blur.
The days that stick will be the ones,
That caused emotions fierce to stir.

You'll remember the rows,
Heartbreak and tears,
The anger and jealousy
That you felt through the years.

You'll remember the love,
That you gave and received,
Those memories will be stronger,
Than you could have believed.

You'll remember the songs,
That accompanied your days,
The emotions they stirred,
Keep your memories ablaze.

The bad days will come,
You can't keep them at bay,
But the good times need chasing,
So they'll come your way.

Don't turn down the invites,
When they're sent your way,
Step away from the work,
And make time to play.

Seek out the love,
Make time for your friends,
Pack in a few parties,
Before this life ends.

Life Laundry

Take pleasure in the small things,
It is the simple life brings peace,
The material world brings stress and strain,
Take time out to find release.
The things that surround our busy lives,
All those possessions we collect,
They clutter up our thoughts and mind,
As round our home they are decked.
So make some space around you,
Have a clear out before spring,
Remove the junk and clutter,
Clear the energy they bring.
To remove the negativity,
That stagnates in your home,
Step outside into the fresh air,
It is time for you to roam.
Search out the works of nature,
That will lift your spirit high,
Seek out the open spaces,
That will let your spirit fly.
The possessions that surround you,
Will overwhelm and drag you down,
So seek some solace in the country,
Away from the stresses of the town.
Let the open spaces lift you
And when you come back home renewed,
Hold on to all the positives
Of the world that you just viewed.
Use the energy raised within you,
To look at your world anew,
And clear out some possessions
That seem to stick to you like glue!

Light Bulb Moment

Enlightenment comes in many forms,
One day the penny drops,
And all those things that troubled us,
Fade away as our world stops.
The trivial, the pointless, the mundane and the chores,
Just aren't important any more, won't open any doors.
We must do something different,
If we are to change our course,
Doing the same things every day,
Will old habits reinforce.
If we make the same mistakes,
We will get the same result,
We won't achieve our hopes or dreams,
Our aspirations we insult.
So break out of your comfort zone,
Go and try something new,
If you've lost sight of what you want,
Go looking for that too.
Sometimes it takes disaster, to shake us from our perch,
As we sleepwalk all the way through life,
Forget we're here to search.
Tragedy brings us focus,
As we realise way too fast,
That our time here is limited,
We were not built to last.
So search for all the answers,
Go out looking for the clues,
Until you find out why you're here,
What have you got to lose?

Live, Love, Laugh.

Laughter is the best medicine, that surely must be true,
There is humour in everything that we feel and see and do.
Sometimes it's hard to find, when our life gives us grief,
But if we seek the humour out we'll get some light relief.
The laughter lifts our mood and picks us up again,
When all we see is fear and all we feel is pain.
You'll find the humour in, the most unlikely place,
Just when you really need it
Spirit will put a smile upon your face.
Make sure you seek out friendship,
From those who'll lift your mood,
Shut out those folks that drag you down,
Don't fear you're being rude.
You do not need the presence,
Of those who sap your strength,
Some need to spread despondency
And they will go to any length
To put their angst on others
And spread misery far and wide,
You really do not need
These miserable buggers by your side.
So seek out those lovely people
Who will lift and bring you cheer,
Let the miserable get on with it
'cause you don't need them near!

Look for the Illusion

There is no such thing as magic; it is not real at all,
We all know it is illusion, intended to enthral.
We try to see the sleight of hand,
To see through all the smoke,
But the very best magicians can fool all of the folk.
So it is with life, some people hide their true intent,
They say they're on your side but their love is only lent.
They are only here to take from you;
They've got nothing to give,
They are out for all that they can get, not here to help you live.
Sometimes it's hard to spot them
They hide themselves so well,
You think you need them by your side
But in fact they make life hell.
If you just look hard at all the folks that are around,
You will learn to spot them for your judgement is quite sound.
Do not be scared to back away from people on the take,
You do not need them in your life so give yourself a break.
Close them out of your affairs, don't let them get a hold,
Let them deal with their own problems,
Make sure that they are told
That they must not sponge off others,
They must earn things for them self,
It is not your job to provide for them,
Be mindful of your health.
Do not fear that they will suffer;
They need to endure the daily grind,
You are not being selfish, just being cruel to be kind!

Magic Words

Magic words fly off the pen, or so it seems to be,
There is no thought of mine involved,
No input comes from me.
The less I think the better, the faster comes each word,
The more I shut my mind away, the more the words are heard.
I must close down all the chatter,
Shut away thoughts of my own,
Let the words drop in from up above as I put my head on loan.
There is no special talent, involved as I proceed,
No equipment's necessary, pen and paper's all I need.
I just need to sit quiet, close my eyes and drift away,
I only need to trust that they will give me things to say.
They never let me down, I write down all I get,
(Though I can't do it in the shower
'Cause the paper gets all wet!)
When I am given something I sometimes get a feel,
Of where it should be going, who my words are meant to heal.
I must trust what I am given, and never be afraid,
To pass on every message after the effort Spirit's made.
The connection it is precious, and should not be denied,
If my target will not take it, at least I know I tried.
But the usual outcome is that the message will be heard,
And that the target will, in fact, hang on to every word.
It may bring them the comfort that they so sorely need,
If I can plant inside their head a seed of hope indeed.

Leaving the Nest

Small child where art thou now?
You've slipped through my fingers one last time.
A grown man now, a child no more,
No longer enrobed in dirt and grime.
Your smile still wide, from ear to ear,
Lights up the room when you appear.
Not often now, does your presence grace
My home and I should not chase
Your company but let you find your own way here.
You've left a hole within these walls,
That I must fill with memories clear,
It is your time to leave this place,
Go forth and make your mark my dear.
Live by the standards I have set,
Don't let them slip, as others tempt you
Away from rules that you know well
Protect you from the lies they tell.
You must take risks, that's how you learn,
Do not be pressured by your peers
Into things that can only end in tears
If not for you then tears for me,
As my child suffers needlessly.
I must let go, let you run free
After so many years protecting you from harm
It's time to let you be,
This does not come easily you know,
A mother's instincts never go.

Make the Best of It

Take time out of the madness,
Cherish those moments well,
They will strengthen and support you
Through another day from hell,
The madness of this world
With its many ups and downs,
Will sap your inner strength
As you deal with fools and clowns
Who think that they can run your life
Much better than yourself,
As they interfere and change the rules
And damage your health and wealth.
They start off meaning well
With plans to improve all things,
But they never foresee the outcomes
That their ill thought plans will bring.
"If we do this, what will happen?"
Is the question they should ask,
And they need to ask it of others
Before they embark upon their task.

They are not blessed with foresight,
These souls who run all things,
They have their own agendas,
Want their fingers in everything.
They cannot accept that most of us
Can run our lives quite well,
We don't need their interference
To make our life a living hell.

We all came here from Spirit
With our own abilities,
And we can manage very nicely
If they would just leave us be.
In the meantime we must be patient
And bear the crosses they inflict,
And try not to get too depressed
When our pockets they have picked,
Make the best of what we have
Is all that we can do,
Take time to enjoy those things for free
With which the Good Lord blesses you.

Making History

Lost in the mists of time,
Corroded, neglected and covered in grime,
The things from our past get lost on the way,
We try to keep them but they will decay.
We hold on to things to keep the memories alive,
Each time we hold them our thoughts they revive,
They help us connect to what has gone before,
To hold on to the knowledge, the past we explore.

We need to connect, to help us feel we belong,
We look to the past, to see where we are from,
We search through the archives, to help us find our place,
We need to know where we fit, in time and in space.
We try to link into, the lives lived before,
To discover the hardships that they did endure,
They say you can't learn from the errors of others,
But nor should we forget what history uncovers.

Making Time

Child of mine, listen well today,
As well as work, make time to play,
As well as toil, make time to sleep,
Make time to laugh, when you would weep.
Make time for friends and family too,
In turn they will make time for you,
Make time for music, listen well,
The notes, truly from heaven fell
Sent for your joy, to uplift you
When life gives you too much to do.
Make time for nature; its wonders vast,
When shadows in your life are cast,
It gives perspective to your woes,
Gives time for thought so answers grow.
Make time for the animal kingdom too,
They will bring so much love to you,
Distract you, when you worry so
About all the answers you don't know.
Make time for love in all its forms,
It will see you through the fiercest storms,
It matters not, what, who or how,
Just love with all your heart and vow
To keep on loving every day,
Whatever pain gets in your way.
So much to do, so little time,
May you find help in this little rhyme.

Mum

My mother is my rock in life, she knows me oh so well,
When something is troubling me she very soon can tell.
She may leave me to deal with it, she will not interfere,
But if I am not coping she always will be here.
She will fight my corner for me, she's always on my side,
She helps me to go forward when I want to run and hide.
She lets me make my own decisions even if they are mistakes,
When it later all goes pear-shaped, her head she never shakes.
She never says "I told you so", she just says "never mind",
As she helps pick up the pieces that I have left behind.
When we are young, we take for granted,
The things that mothers do,
We just assume they'll help us deal
With all the trouble that we brew.
Once we have children of our own the penny finally drops,
We are responsible for someone's life,
With us the buck now stops.
That prospect takes our breath away as we finally realise,
And start to look instead,
At the world through our mother's eyes.

No Fear

There is nothing to fear but fear itself,
It invades our mind and affects our health.

We fear for the future, we fear ghosts from our past,
Some fear every day will be their last.

Some fear the dark and the shadows of night,
Some fear to step forward into the light.

We fear what life's bringing, we fear the unknown,
When we worry too much we find our fears have grown.

But fear serves little purpose, it just holds us back,
It may prevent us from moving along our life's track.

Our fears and our phobias just exist in our mind,
If we really try hard we can leave them behind.

In order to move on from our fears we just must,
Remember that Spirit is there and just trust.

It will never send things with which we cannot cope,
So cast off your fears and move forward with hope.

No Time Like the Present

What would you do with your very last day?
Would you spend it at work or spend it at play?
Would you spend it with loved ones or spend time alone?
Would you break a few rules before it's time to go home?
This could be your last chance to live out your dreams,
Your last opportunity to go to extremes.
Just push out the boat as you go for broke,
You've nothing to lose so give the boundaries a poke.
Make sure that there's nothing that you've left unsaid,
Make sure that all hatchets are buried and dead.
If you've fallen out with someone you once loved,
Make sure you make peace, don't leave them unloved.
Don't let the miserable spoil your very last day,
Spend it with the cheerful, send the moaners away.
Don't get bogged down with the trivial and mundane,
They waste so much time for so little gain.
Look for the big things to do to fulfil,
All your hopes and your dreams and give one last great thrill.
Call up your friends and your loved ones to see,
If they'll join you for one last, huge, jamboree.
Now none of us know when this day will arrive,
We assume that tomorrow we'll still be alive.
But this may not be so because life goes so fast,
So live every day as if it's your last!

No Worries

Give your worries to the Angels,
Send your worries to the stars.
Set yourself free from your prison,
Self-imposed, it has no bars.
Plagued by life's anxieties,
By thoughts you've come to dread.
You cannot see the wood for trees,
You are trapped in your own head.

You are free to leave its walls
Any time your soul doth choose,
Take yourself away from worries,
That you find you cannot lose.
Worry serves no purpose,
It will paralyse your mind,
Will prevent you moving forward,
Make you deaf and dumb and blind.

You will not hear the answers
That the Angels try to send,
You will forget to ask them questions
That could see your worries end.
You will not see the clues they leave
So you can see the light,
Give your worries to the Angels,
So you can sleep at night!

Nothing Wasted

Any moment, any time,
Life could change, turn on a dime.
You think your path is set in stone,
The plans you've made all quite your own.

One day, the applecart gets turned,
The unforeseen leaves all plans burned.
But life goes on, the wheels still turn,
You pause, regroup, a lesson learn.

Two steps forward, one step back,
As life goes on you get the knack,
Of dealing with, all that gets thrown,
Before you know it, find you've grown.

So don't be scared of what life brings,
The challenges that make life sting,
They'll slow you down, just for a while,
Then on you'll go, it's all worthwhile.

One Day at a Time

One day at a time, are the words that they give you,
When times are so hard it's the best of advice.
Don't think far ahead for the prospect will scare you,
Just get through today is enough to suffice.
So much to deal with it just overwhelms you,
You are drowning in tasks that you cannot get done.
The harder you try the deeper you sink down,
Like quicksand it traps you, leaves no time for fun.
Step back for a while; take time for a breather,
Do something you love again, just for a while.
It will build up your energy, renew and complete you,
Give you strength that you need to help deal with your trial.
You will find then the tasks become less all-consuming,
You can start to tick them all off one by one.
Make sure that you ask for some help with your burden,
And always make sure you make time to have fun!

Onwards and Upwards

You cannot see forever, you can only see the now,
You cannot tell how long you've got,
Before you take your bow.
Learn from every minute, look for the lessons from the day,
There is a point to everything, though it may not feel that way.

The trials and tribulations that you are sent to face,
Are only those that you picked out
Before you joined the human race,
The things you think you cannot face
Are tests beyond compare,
Spirit gives you strength, so face them head on if you dare.

You may be sent to places, where you can do no right,
Be put in situations, where you can't win the fight.
Sometimes the things you do, will hurt the ones you love,
But be true to your instincts and take guidance from above.

Try not to act on impulse,
Consider the outcome of your deeds,
When you choose your path in life, consider others' needs.
Try not to leave too much destruction in your wake,
And as you go along, try to give more than you take.

Sometimes the acts of others, will turn life upside down,
And instead of treading water, you feel yourself start to drown.
It seems unfair when the situation, is not one that you made,
To have to cope with the fallout, when it rains on your parade.

Deal with what life throws at you, and do it with good grace,
Don't resent the challenges, that you are sent to face,
When you've finished clearing up the mess,
You'll see the total sum
Of all the things that you've just learned,
And see how far you've come.

Patience is a Virtue

Time is a great healer, so we are always told,
But oh, it takes so long to come in from the cold
When we have lost a loved one, we feel we'll never lose
That emptiness inside us, that fills us with the blues.

The time goes by so slowly, when we are left alone,
The heart that beats inside us, feels like it's made of stone.
But it will still keep beating, we have to carry on,
We must fulfil our purpose, even though our love has gone.

Spirit will be with us, it will lead us by the hand,
And on the darkest days, will hold us up when we can't stand.
There's more for us to do, it may be teach, it may be learn,
We must not pass to Spirit, until it is our turn.

So if ever we are tempted, to speed up that passing on,
We must learn to be patient, for our tasks are not all done.
We cannot rush the lessons, they must all be learned,
Then we will truly know our place in Spirit has been earned!

Positive Connections

What motivates you every day?
What drives you on your earthly way?
What makes you do the things you do?
How much do you do for you?
Are you motivated by the need
To make sure you've enough to feed
Your offspring and assorted pets,
And pay extortionate bills from vets?
You plough through every single day,
There are so many bills to pay.
There is no time to dwell upon
Your spiritual needs, your 'me' time's gone.
But Spirit walks with you every day
Your whole life through, each step of the way.
You can bring Spirit in to all that you do,
As you dwell on the needs of those around you.
It may be something simple like holding a door,
To make an old lady's struggle less of a chore.
Pass the time of day while you're stuck in a queue,
With the lonely old man who is stuck behind you.
There is always a chance that you just may,
Be the only person he speaks to today.
Be mindful of all, don't walk round in a daze,
You can make a difference in so many ways.
Connect with the world with a nod and a smile,
It will come back to you and make your life worthwhile.
Your spirit will grow and be strengthened for sure,
By all the connections that you made time for.

Progress

Let us illuminate the path before you,
Light the road that you might see your way,
There us far that you still need to travel,
Be sure to go a little further every day.
You may pause a while to catch your breath and ponder,
On all the things that you have seen so far,
Not all has been a smooth and happy journey,
Not every day that you would shout hurrah.
But you have learned much more than most the others,
As you bravely climb the rocks that strew your path,
When others would fall down and sit and cry dear,
You will rise again and turn and laugh.
You will ignore the pains that plague you,
Won't let them hold you back from moving on,
You will continue on the path you chose dear,
Long after weaker souls have given up and gone.
Rewards will come to those who persevere dear,
We will not let your efforts go unseen,
We watch and guide you every single step dear,
As we follow to all the places you have been.
With your determination and forbearance,
You will overcome all problems in your way,
You will never know how proudly we observe you,
Just make sure you make some progress every day.

Relative Abilities

How the birds of the air must pity us,
As we walk upon the land,
They look down from above, flying when we can only stand.
They travel in 3D, soaring up, down and left and right,
They laugh at the cumbersome things we build,
As we seek to reach their height.
They just cannot imagine how restricted we must feel,
For them, just walking on two legs, it has no real appeal.
The many fish within the sea must look at us and stare,
They cannot imagine how we cope just living in the air,
We cannot exist under the waves without tanks upon our back,
The fish look on and pity the ability we lack.
So we should not judge others by what they can or cannot do,
Those less able than ourselves achieve fulfilment too.
They do not need our pity as we look at them and stare,
We would not want the pity of the birds up in the air.
Their challenges are greater
Than those more able-bodied souls,
The path that they must follow has no short cuts to their goals.
But their spirit will develop so much faster than the rest,
They will score a higher grade because they take a harder test.
We should lend a helping hand
To those who find their lives so tough.
And we should count our blessings
That our path is not so rough.

Riches Indeed

A clever man once said to me,
"There is gold buried there under that tree.
You go and look and you will see,
Look for yourself, don't take it from me."
Well I dug and dug and I couldn't find,
But I couldn't get his words out of my mind,
I passed that way again in spring,
And what did I find to make my heart sing?
A swaying sea of yellow and gold,
A marvellous sight 'twas to behold,
A fanfare of trumpets filled that place,
As the daffodils of spring greet my sweet face.

Given the infinite nature of time and space being within ten minutes and half a mile of a specified time and place is nothing short of a miracle.

Ted Tester

Right Time, Right Place

How does it come together, the results of Spirit's plan?
Is there a big control room, staffed by a little man?
He has to know the whereabouts of every single being,
As he tries to plot our movements, all hearing and all seeing.
His task, to bring together, those who are supposed to meet,
To fulfil their chosen destiny, to make their life complete.
He has fingers in all pies, he must juggle like no other,
To connect up every father with the most appropriate mother.

He can see all of the little stuff, is always on the case,
When he needs to put somebody in exactly the right place.
Life's timing it is crucial when you're trying to meet your fate,
It is no good being in the right place
If you're there ten minutes late.
When things don't happen fast enough for us upon this plane,
There is always a good reason, though it feels like such a pain.
He is trying to make it happen,
Though it feels like it won't ever,
He must get so excited when a plan does come together.

And so we must be patient as we wait for life to move,
When something is preventing us as we're stuck in a groove.
Give the man a little credit, see how vast his enterprise,
Sometimes to make things happen
Will take more than a few tries.
Make sure you do your bit, don't just sit at home and wait,
You will have to make some effort if you are to meet your fate.
Cut the man a little slack and know he does his very best,
There is much goes on behind the scenes,
He never gets to rest!

Small Cog in a Big Wheel.

I'm totally here, I'm totally there,
I'm completely, absolutely, everywhere.
There is no place I have not been,
Nothing at all I have not seen.
It's all in me, every last little thing,
I'm connected by Spirit to everything.

In this incarnation I feel very small,
I can't comprehend the size of it all.
I've only been given a small role to play,
A very small cog in a big wheel I'd say.
I cannot bring with me all I learned before,
And I cannot go back until I've learned some more.

It would be so easy if I could just see,
All the answers that already lie within me.
But there's no fun in cheating, the game I must play,
I am here for a reason, to learn more each day.
I can reach back inside; get a glimpse of my soul,
But I must move forwards 'til I reach my goal.

Soldiers of the Light

Soldiers of the light are we,
Solid, dependable, born to think free.
No doctrine controls us, no dogma, no creed,
We will bring to you whatever you need.
We will lift and enfold you, bring comfort, end fears,
And if you are sad we will share in your tears.
We are there when you need us, if you're feeling alone,
You can bend all our ears if you need to moan.

We'll help you pick up the pieces when life leaves you broke,
If you need to laugh then we'll tell you a joke.
You can join us for life, or just for a while,
Pop in when you need us, when life is a trial.
While you are here feel your loved ones draw close,
Don't forget we'll be here when you need us most.
Draw strength from our comfort, our words and our love,
And know those that you miss watch o'er you from above.

Solitude

Solitude should not be avoided,
It allows us some time just to think,
When the stresses of life overwhelm us,
It can pull us right back from the brink.
Put our thoughts and our dreams in some order,
Choose the things that we want to do first,
Get rid of stuff needed no longer,
'Cause otherwise our head will burst.

You can be alone without being lonely,
Do not fear to spend time on your own,
Turn off all the things that distract you,
Let thoughts grow from the seeds you have sown.
Your life will stagnate and not progress,
If you never stop, to think about you,
If you spend all your time with the others,
You'll keep doing what they want you to do.

They will heap all their troubles upon you,
Only let their agenda be read,
You will have no time left to listen,
To ideas Spirit puts in your head.
The plan for your life is all in there,
It was put in place before you came,
But if you do not open the gateway,
Then you'll keep on just doing the same.

Tell the Truth

Shelter here awhile, let us protect you while you heal,
Let us explain life's mysteries as its truths we now reveal.
Let us remove confusion, let us remove all doubt,
As we provide the evidence of what life's all about.

Don't give us faith, there is no need, don't swallow every word,
Don't follow our teachings blindly
Just because it's what you heard.
Make up your mind all on your own;
Seek the proof for what we say,
We will provide the evidence for you to take away.
Ponder a while on what you've heard, examine and dissect,
When you are sure that it is true then give us due respect.

Tell others of the things you've heard,
That they may see truth too,
Bring them to us that we may help them
Change their point of view.
Let us open up their minds to possibilities once unknown,
Let us bring comfort, remove all fear as the evidence is shown.
Let them too in their turn go forth
And spread truth far and wide,
When you need guidance for yourself
Learn to listen to the voice inside.

The Ancestors

Mention my name, don't forget that I was here,
Talk about me often and it will bring me near,
Keep my memory alive by telling the younger ones of me,
Teach them all the history of our little family.
Make sure you show them pictures,
Make some copies they can keep,
Tell them stories of the days gone by before they go to sleep.
They should know where they have come from, let them know where they belong,
It will root them in this family and keep them feeling strong.
Draw the family tree for them,
Use a computer if you must,
It will make the names seem real to them, not just bodies turned to dust.

We ancestors watch over them, we help them on their way,
Please tell them who we are
And that they will meet us one day!

Only the Good...

Candles in the wind have flames that flicker, twist and turn,
They are vulnerable and fragile, not sure how long they'll burn.
So it is with some souls as they travel in this sphere,
There are no guarantees of how long they will be here.
Their behaviour can be reckless,
Their regard for safety sadly lacks,
Their friends and loved ones watching over them,
Make sure they've got their backs.
But even with this assistance it is hard to keep them safe,
They are not meant to be here long
So when they leave do not lose faith.
They are fulfilling their own destiny;
This path was theirs to take,
You could not stop it happening,
This choice was theirs to make.
Do not feel guilt you were not there
When the wrong choices were made,
Just keep them close inside your heart,
The memories won't fade.

The Art of Mediation

Sometimes in life it seems to me,
There are no right answers to dilemmas that we see,
We are stuck in the middle trying to be strong,
With no right answers, only different shades of wrong.
When people that we love fall out
We are torn between the two,
We could take sides but always
There will be two points of view,
How do we know who's wrong or right
Or if only one's to blame?
They both will see things differently, never both the same.

If we sit upon the fence we will fall out with them both,
So should we just side with the one we like the most?
We could just turn our backs when we can't make a choice,
And we can't face the fallout if our opinions we do voice,
But that is not the answer, it's the lazy person's way,
Surely we can find a tactful way to have our say?
If we are a true friend we must do what's for the best,
If we desert them in their hour of need
They will not be impressed.

Don't play piggy in the middle, shuttling to and fro,
Saying "he said this" or "she said that" is not the way to go.
It's like playing Chinese whispers and the message will distort,
And if they just shoot the messenger
Your efforts are for nought!
They should be talking to each other, not to everyone around,
If you can make that happen maybe progress can be found.
Lack of communication can be the cause of much distress,
Often misunderstandings are the reason for the mess.

If we look back in history, at all that's gone before,
Poor communication can lead to a state of war,
Things get out of hand so quickly, soon there's no going back,
There may be a simple explanation
That would get things back on track.
It may be that all they need is someone to referee,
Help them explore the argument until they can agree.
If you rise to this challenge, but a truce you can't deliver,
Maybe you could persuade them both to just agree to differ!

The Case for Reincarnation

I'm curious, it must be said,
To know what happens once I'm dead.
Does everything stop and it all goes black,
Once I've gone is there no coming back?
Maybe the atheists have it sussed,
And once we have gone we leave just dust.
But if that's true then what's the point,
Of all that happens in this joint?

Why make the effort to behave,
Be good, be honest, loyal and brave?
There'd be nought to gain from all we did,
No behaviour that we would forbid.
No lessons for us to take away,
No consequences at the end of the day.
I can't believe that there's not more,
Else what on earth was it all for?

So once we've drawn our final breath,
I'm sure there exists life after death.
But we can't know what form it takes,
Is there punishment for our mistakes?
The carrot and the stick approach has served Christianity well.
If you're good there's heaven, and if you're not there's hell.
What a great incentive, to make people behave,
As they travel on their way from the cradle to the grave.

Young me didn't need religion, I thought I knew it all,
I could not see the point of believing in a god at all.
I was so focussed on myself I surely could not see,
That there was a bigger picture
Which was not just all about me.

The consequences of my actions as I passed along my way,
Were no concern of mine, I thought I was only here to play.
But with growing age came wisdom,
And with it conscience too,
I realised there was more to life, including other points of view.

As I look around this Earth it is surely plain to see,
That we are all at different stages as we develop spiritually.
Just one lifetime can't be enough to learn all that we must,
To progress to the level of the souls that simply just
Are way above the rest of us, they exude peace and love,
They cope with every ordeal that is sent down from above.
While the rest of us are struggling with what life has in store,
They make the hard look easy,
Surely they've done it all before?

We learn so much while we are here, it should not go to waste,
Surely we take it with us, when with the end we're faced?
Material things don't matter, we must leave them all behind,
But I'm sure we get to take all of the contents of our mind.
And if old age has stopped us, remembering all we knew,
I know that it's all locked inside, awaiting pastures new.
So when our time is over, and all the answers we have found,
Perhaps we'll take a break before we play another round!

The Engineers

So clever, these little men. They come, they mend,
Things you sometimes did not know were broken.
They work away, behind closed doors,
Leaving all things fixed and new, with words unspoken.

Talented, it's true; with gifts that others
Only dare to dream exist.
When others would give up and walk away,
They will still persist.

They will not fail, refuse to see, insoluble problems
That lesser men will not engage,
'Plough on', their mantra, with tasks
That would leave less patient souls enraged.

What gives these souls the patience of a saint,
The perseverance to succeed?
They work for love, not for recognition, reward or greed.

A job well done is their reward,
A person helped, an object mended,
A project no one else would touch,
A building built, a garden tended.

A challenge they can rise to inspires their mind,
Drives them on until their task us done,
They love the insurmountable,
The impossible is their idea of fun.

These are the special ones, the ones we send
To make a difference on this Earth,
Their path is written, laid out before them,
From the moment of their birth.

Guard these souls well; let them inspire you too,
Without them, man would never tackle something new.

The Guide

Feel my arms around you, let me lift you when you fall.
Let me ease the path before you, I will hear you when you call.

Do not fear the journey, the path is one you chose,
I will follow close behind you, every step that your soul goes.
When your feet get weary, I will carry you a while.
Until once again you're ready, to walk another mile.

Though sometimes you are lonely, you are never on your own.
I am always here beside you, I will not leave you alone.

You may never feel my presence,
You may never hear my voice,
But I am watching over you, to be here is my choice.

I will not interfere, I only help you when you ask,
So when you start to struggle, let me help you with your task.
I cannot do it for you, that was never my intent,
The guidance may be gentle, but it surely will be sent.

The Guiding Light

There manifests itself a light,
It's not so big, it's not so bright,
A tiny glow inside our heart,
Where spirit dwells right from the start.
It travels everywhere we go,
It never, ever leaves us, though
There may be times it's hard to find,
When we push Spirit from our mind.
Our lives are cold and empty then,
We are just shadows waiting, when
One day the happenings in our lives,
Means we call Spirit to our side.
The light that dwells within us, then
Will manifest itself again,
It grows and fills that gaping hole,
Illuminating heart and soul.
The strength it brings will just astound,
Our capabilities know no bounds,
The clarity of thought it brings,
Allows us to deal with anything.
When the crises pass we look back at length,
And wonder where we found the strength,
To deal with such enormous things,
But that's the strength that Spirit brings.
You can be this strong all the time,
To ask for help is not a crime,
Keep Spirit with you all the while,
Don't save it 'til disasters pile
Upon you and you cannot cope,
Look for the light that gives you hope,
When next you need help with the fight,
Just let your spirit lamp burn bright.

The Meaning of Dreaming

Quietly into the night I go,
Let the waves of sleep wash over me,
I travel far away, to places I will never be,
I escape from reality a while, engage with other souls,
Take a step aside from trying to reach impossible goals.
The stresses of the day depart and my mind becomes my own,
No interruptions to my thoughts as tiny seeds are sown.
The starting point for many things are revealed while I sleep,
The clues to get me through the day
And the trials that make me weep.
I should trust these dreams of mine the answers to provide,
As these little pearls of wisdom are dripped in from outside.
My day is oh so busy I could never find the time,
To see the clues before me and to act upon the signs,
But the night brings opportunities
That the day declines to find,
As I open up to the realms above the dark corners of my mind.
Just as my computer, does its updates as it must,
I download information, that I must learn to trust.
If I find my dreams repeat, I have ignored the message sent,
I must play them back again to work out what was meant,
Eventually, the penny drops and I move on once more,
Making progress through my life
With help provided while I snore.

The Art of Reconciliation

"To err is human; to forgive, divine,"
Three centuries old, is this famous line.
To forgive and forget would help us move on,
When we have been wronged and our trust is gone.
It would be so easy if we could just let things go,
Leave the hurt all behind and get on with the show.
But it's harder to do, than it is to say,
We could hold on to our grudges 'til our dying day.

Our hurt and our anger goes round in our head,
We go over and over what was done or was said.
Sometimes we will even seek out revenge,
As our humiliation or hurt we try to avenge.
The person who suffers the most in this case,
Is the one who is trying so hard to save face.
The damage hate does to our mind and our soul,
Can prevent us from reaching our chosen life's goal.

So how do we manage to forgive and move on,
What will change the mind that we're so set upon?
We must try to see the opposite side,
Understand their motives and swallow our pride,
Realise that everyone makes their mistakes,
Accept no-one's perfect for everyone's sakes,
Forgive for yourself, leave no room for regret,
And if you cannot forgive, at least try to forget!

The Real Me

Moments of the past come back to me,
As clear now as they were then.
Flashes of times gone by,
When girls were girls and men were men.
I had no choice then in the path I took,
But now I wouldn't get a second look,
Could be how I feel, not trapped in a shell,
That made my life such a living hell.
I buried it deep, the real me inside,
I found a wife, who stayed by my side.
She never knew my life was a lie,
She bore me three sons and a girl by and by.
But it all felt so wrong this life that I led,
I couldn't be who I was in my head,
My secret stay hid, I didn't dare let it out,
The penalties then left me in no doubt
That I would suffer much more if I revealed who I was,
I would be beaten and spat on and all just because
I didn't love as the world said that I should,
But was I really so evil when I only did good?

I never betrayed my wife, though I wanted to so,
She was always my best friend and I did love her, though
Not as she should be, a woman that fine
Deserved love and romance, not a love that's a lie.
I don't know if she knew I was not what she saw,
What I wanted to be was against every law,
Both the church and the state thought I should be cured,
That my life was an illness to be hidden and endured.
The stigma attached made me keep my heart closed,
I could not face the world if my lie was exposed.
But how times have changed, now I could live with my truth,
I could love with my heart from the start of my youth,
Society now accepts all kinds of souls,
Lets us love who we want and fulfil all our roles.
Be brave, those like me, step into your shoes,
And find someone to love now you've nothing to lose.

The Self Destruct Button

We are programmed, sometimes, to self-destruct,
To blow our world apart,
We don't know why we do it, but it's in us from the start.
We're jogging on quite nicely, with all things going well,
When we do something stupid and make our life a living hell.
We usually know we've done it, we made a conscious choice,
We thought that we knew best so we ignored that little voice
That dwells within our mind
And keeps us on the straight and narrow,
Doing boring stuff like fishing and growing vegetable marrow.
We think that we have stuffed things up
But really we learn loads,
We pack in so many lessons every time our world implodes.
But we should try to remember all the lessons that we learned,
We don't need to repeat the times we got our fingers burned.
Learn once, learn well and move along
To the lesson that comes next,
If you don't crack it this time
Life could be permanently wrecked.
Sometimes there's no way back
When too much damage has been done,
The loved ones that surround you back away when you're no
fun.

Don't drive them all away or try to drag them down with you,
They can see what you're doing but can't live your life for you.
They cannot deal with what they see when you are such a pain,
So they will stay away until you've fixed yourself again.
Only you can turn it round and you know what to do,
You must discard old habits that bring so much harm to you.
You have so much to give inside, so much that you can share,
Don't let it all get buried by the demons that dwell there.
'Tis time to drive them out, this time once and for all,
Learn this lesson for the last time, ask for help and you won't fall.

The Tour Guide

Guided by us, but led by you,
Along the path of life so new.
We can only work within the rules,
We send you help, we give you tools.
When you are new you cannot see,
That for every lock, we send the key.
It's always there but tucked away,
To help you with the game you play.
We see that you go round and round
In circles, 'til the key is found.
Sometimes it takes you oh, so long,
So many times, you get it wrong.
We stand and cheer you from the side,
And we can see how hard you tried.
We'd love to do your tasks for you,
We even try to send a clue,
But oft you miss the help we send,
You'd drive the Saints around the bend.
How much frustration must we stand,
As you fail again to take our hand?
But as you age the wisdom grows,
The lessons learned, experience shows.
You learn not to repeat mistakes,
And we don't mind how long it takes.
You can have all the time you need,
Lessons repeat, 'til you take heed.
And when the penny finally drops,
Our job is done, the lessons stop.
Your Spirit needs no more, to roam,
And we will come, to take you home.

Time Out

Carry the memories with you, of all that has gone before,
Take them out and polish them,
And then go make some more.
The world it doesn't stop, just when you think it would,
It keeps spinning on its axis
And time keeps ticking like it should.
You want to sit so quietly and just be left alone,
No knocking on the door and no-one ringing on the phone.
Turn the telly off and shut the world outside away,
Just sit a while in silence and listen to your thoughts today.
Take some time away from living and take time just to be,
Put some space around you and let your mind run free.
Let the healing space created soothe and lift your soul,
Soon you will start feeling that you are back in control.
The world it whizzes round us makes us dizzy and confused,
The events thrown at us, leave us battered, tired and bruised.
If our body becomes injured we allow it time to heal,
Don't expect it to climb mountains
When with pain it has to deal.
We should show our mind the same respect
When trauma comes our way,
Feed it love and understanding;
Don't just push on through the day.
Take some time away from all the many troubles you can see,
Your mind will thank you for some space
And you'll preserve your sanity.

To Be, or Not to Be? That is the Question:

Sometimes take time away from 'do'
And spend time just to 'be'.
Though 'do' enables us to learn 'be' enables us to see.
It also lets us listen and taste and smell and feel,
Engages us with senses that make this world feel real.
If you spend your time just doing,
You will miss most of the ride,
Like riding a roller-coaster with your eyes shut, petrified.
Spirit gave you senses, to enhance your journey here.
If you are blessed to have them all, engage them without fear.
Don't fear the sights your eyes will see or the words your ears will hear.
Don't close the world around you out,
Don't be scared to shed a tear.
It is easy to stay busy, in this world that moves so fast,
Spend all your day just doing from the first hour to the last.
Take time to reflect upon the things that you have done,
Examine how they make you feel, was any of it fun?
What did you do for you today? Was it all for others' gain?
What did you feel as the day went on?
How much of it was pain?
Your path will never change if you don't examine how you feel,
Don't bury yourself in 'doing' see what 'being' can reveal.

Trust in the Journey

One up, one down, one laugh, one frown,
One smile, one tear, one love, one fear,
One rage, one calm, one safe from harm,
So many ways that we can be,
What will this day now hold for me?

Some wake with fear, their path not clear,
Their destiny, not theirs to see,
Others intrude, control their mood,
As they impose upon those souls,
Their will, their power, their own sad goals.

With life not theirs, they turn to prayers,
To see if they, can change the way,
That life proceeds, to meet their needs.

Prayers have the power to change all things,
When we struggle with the challenges life brings.

The answers come, quite clear for some,
But others find, their state of mind,
Prevents the flow, they must let go
Of fear, of hate, loathing, disgust,
Just learn to love, just learn to trust.

Two Minds

Inside my head two people fight,
One does what's wrong, one does what's right.
Just when I think that good will win,
The evil one commits more sin.
I try each day as I begin,
To suffocate the evil twin.
To deprive it of the food it needs,
Of hate, of jealousy and of greed.
I try to feed the good in me,
With love, with hope, with charity.
But as the day proceeds I find,
The evil one invades my mind.
The things that others do to me,
Will cloud my thoughts and purity.
Emotions will come into play,
That allow the evil twin his say.

His little voice inside my head,
Gives rise to feelings that I dread.
I find my tongue says things that may
Hurt others that I meet today.
My actions too, betray my soul,
As I fail again to reach my goal.
Why is it so hard to be good?
To do the things we know we should?
We know as soon as the deed is done,
That we should have stopped and not begun.
The trick is learn to recognise,
The evil twin when his voice lies
That something is a good idea,
Don't allow his thoughts to commandeer
Your own. Seek out the good in you,
It's always there, let it shine through.

Unconditional Love

Our capacity for love it knows no bounds,
Unconditional love is just what it sounds,
We never run out, we always have more,
We turn on the tap and out it will pour.
When we truly love them, then it matters not
What they do to us, not one little jot.
If they hurt us or harm us, inflict pain or despair,
Then we will still love them, we will still be there.

We will protect and provide from their moment of birth,
We would go to their aid at the ends of the Earth,
Our animal instincts defy every law,
If our offspring are threatened out comes the claw.
You can legislate rules 'til you're blue in the face,
You can't stop me protecting my gift to this race.
So though I may look oh so meek and so mild,
God help the one comes twixt mother and child!

The Spirit Within

As individuals on the earth plane we often feel lonely and isolated.
These are human emotions not known in the world of Spirit.
In Spirit we do not exist in isolation.
We are part of a group consciousness, all knowing, all seeing.
As humans this can be a mind boggling concept to get our heads round.

The idea that we link to every living thing in some way, whether plant, animal or human is a mind blowing thought.
In Spirit we know all things at all times.
We can link to any part of the consciousness.
Here on earth we are an isolated part of that consciousness.
But we have within the ability to link back in to that state.
When we meditate we go back within ourselves and can link with all things that have gone before, those that are now and those that will be.

Humans like to think of their gods as powerful entities, separate from mere mortals.
All knowing, all seeing with the power to control our destiny.
Beings to be worshipped, feared and ruled by as our religious leaders tell us the rules our gods want us to obey.
But the truth is much simpler than the complicated world we have created in our isolated state.
We are our own gods.
We come from Spirit, we return to Spirit, we are Spirit.

Honesty

Sometimes the hardest person to be honest with is ourselves. We tell ourselves that we are fine and that our life proceeds according to plan.

We do not look inside our minds to seek the unfulfilled dreams of our youth.

So many things we planned to do before the realities of life took over.
How the plans of others around us crushed our own dreams as we sought to make others happy before ourselves.
The things we planned to learn, to experience, to feel, washed away by the tide of life.

Sometimes we spend so much time pleasing others that it becomes our reason to be.

We find our fulfilment in making others happy, our parents, our partners, our children, our friends.

Although bringing happiness to others is rewarding in so many ways it is not why we came.

In being people pleasers we are not being our true, authentic self.

The more we try to please people the more demands will be placed upon us as those around us fail to learn their own lessons, solve their own problems, fulfil their own desires.

Do not be frightened that you will offend someone by saying no to their demands.

You are not responsible for the happiness of others.

Be honest with yourself about what you want from your life.
Be honest with others when they place unreasonable demands upon you.

Be honest and others will respect you for it.
Look inside yourself to find your unfulfilled dreams before it is too late.

Make sure you do something every day that is just for you.

Hotel Eden

We welcome you to Earth today,
We hope that you enjoy your stay,
Your journey here took quite a time,
Around nine months I think you'll find.
Now we have for you to peruse,
A helpful list of don'ts and dos,
A guide to help you get the best
From your stay here as our guest.

Our facilities are second to none,
So make sure that you have some fun.
Take care of those you choose to use,
Use them well but don't abuse.
Our beaches run for miles and miles,
Around our large and tiny isles,
Feel free to use them night and day,
Make sure you play during your stay.

The seas that lap these many shores,
You also can regard as yours,
They teem with life of many kinds,
A menu vast for you to find.
Be sure to keep these waters clean,
Don't make it obvious where you've been,
Allow the life time to recharge,
If you wish to keep your menu large.

Our gardens stretch across the land
Use them to help you understand,
How nature makes things grow for you,
Our menu here's extensive too.
We've every food you could desire,
All the nourishment you could require,
And if it's healing that you seek
Our plants will help you when you're weak.

We have everything that you could need,
To make any beverage indeed,
Tea or coffee by the cup
When you need a pick-me-up
And if you would like a wine that's fine,
Just learn to cultivate the vine.
But don't consume it to excess,
As this may cause you some distress.

We can provide many differing climes,
From icy depths to heat sublime,
Howling gales to days so still,
Swirling snow to make you chill,
Blistering sun or tropical rain,
We try our best to entertain.
If you don't like what we've arranged,
Just wait a while, it's sure to change.

(Cont...)

If you need company while you're here,
There's plenty to choose from, never fear,
There are many guests for you to meet,
To help you make your stay complete,
Some you'll like and some you won't,
Some you'll love and some you don't.
Learn all you can, that's why you're here,
Rise to the challenges that appear.

Now if you look to the sky at night,
The heavens light up for your delight.
Look up and wonder from whence you came,
As you visit Earth playing life's little game,
Enjoy your time here, it goes so fast,
Live every day like it's your last,
Then when your stay is done and you've had your fill,
All this is free....there is no bill.

ALL PROFITS from this Book are being donated to the

Hastings Spiritualist Brotherhood Church

www.HastingsSNU.com

Facebook.com/HastingsSNU

#HastingsSNU

HASTINGS SPIRITUALIST BROTHERHOOD CHURCH

All Welcome Every Friday
7:30pm—9pm
(Doors Open at 7pm)

Weekly Mediumship
Service and Demonstration

£4.00 on the door
£3.50 for members

Prices subject to change

Come along and join us for a wonderful evening of Mediumship in the company of friends. Feel free to stay behind for a cuppa and make new friends in a warm and welcoming atmosphere.

Healing is available during the evening by our team of wonderful, well trained SNU Healing Mediums.

Quaker Meeting House
5 South Terrace, Hastings TN34 1SA
Tel. 01424 218954

SPIRITUALISTS' NATIONAL UNION
LIGHT NATURE TRUTH
AFFILIATED BODY